T A L K

T A L K

CARL HANCOCK RUX

THEATRE COMMUNICATIONS GROUP
NEW YORK
2004

Talk is published by Theatre Communications Group, Inc.,
520 Eighth Avenue, 24th Floor, New York, NY 10018–4156

This publication is made possible in part with public funds from
the New York State Council on the Arts, a State Agency.

This publication of *Talk* has been supported by the Jerome Foundation
in celebration of the Jerome Hill Centennial and in recognition of the
valuable cultural contributions of artists to society.

TCG books are exclusively distributed to the book trade by Consortium
Book Sales and Distribution, 1045 Westgate Dr., St. Paul, MN 55114.

LIBRARY OF CONGRESS CATALOGING-IN-PUBLICATION DATA
Rux, Carl Hancock.
Talk / by Carl Hancock Rux.
p. cm.
Includes bibliographical references and index.
ISBN 1-55936-226-X (pbk. : alk. paper)
1. Congresses and conventions—Drama. 2. African American authors—
Drama. 3. Canon (Literature)—Drama. 4. Critics—Drama.
I. Title.
PS3568.U86 T35   2003
812'.54—dc22   2003015697

Cover design by Mark Melnick
Author photo by Felicia Megginson
Text design and composition by Lisa Govan

First Edition, December 2004

EPIGRAPH

Writing is a self-disturbed activity: it knows itself to be, at once, trivial and apocalyptic, vain yet of the greatest consciousness-altering potential.

—MAURICE BLANCHOT

CONTENTS

TALK

Talk was commissioned by The Foundry Theatre in New York City (Melanie Joseph, Producing Artistic Director) and further developed at The Sundance Theatre Laboratory in 2001. It was directed by Melanie Joseph, with dramaturgy by Jocelyn Clarke. The cast was as follows:

THE MODERATOR	Anthony Mackie
ION	James Himelsbach
MENO	John Seitz
CRITO	Chris McKinney
PHAEDO	Helen Carey
APOLLODOROS	Stephanie Berry

Talk was first produced by The Foundry Theatre at The Joseph Papp Public Theater/New York Shakespeare Festival in March 2002. It was directed by Marion McClinton, the set design was by James Noone, costumes were by Toni-Leslie James, the lighting design was by James L. Vermeulen, the video was by Marilys Ernst and the sound design and music supervision were by Tim Schellenbaum. The dramaturg was Jocelyn Clarke and the production stage manager was Scott Pegg. The cast was as follows:

THE MODERATOR	Anthony Mackie
ION	James Himelsbach
MENO	John Seitz
CRITO	Reg E. Cathey
PHAEDO	Maria Tucci
APOLLODOROS	Karen Kandel

Talk opened at Theater X (David Ravel, Producing Director) in Milwaukee, Wisconsin, in January 2003. It was directed by Dave Ravel. The set and light design was by Stephen Hudson-Mairet, the pottery design was by Thomas Everts, the sound design was by David Elmer and the video was by Marilys Ernst. The cast was as follows:

THE MODERATOR	Timmy Tamisiea
ION	Tom Reed
MENO	John Schneider
CRITO	Rodd Walker
PHAEDO	Flora Coker
APOLLODOROS	Azeeza Islam

CHARACTERS

THE MODERATOR
Young academic. Coordinator and conductor of these sessions.

ION
Award-winning literary critic, lecturer of post-modernist cultural aesthetics, biographer.

MENO
Retired TV talk show host. Ex-vaudevillian.

CRITO
Neoclassicist jazz musician, composer/arranger.
Vietnam veteran.

PHAEDO
Actress, experimental filmmaker.
Professor of Film Studies and the French New Wave.

APOLLODOROS
Performance artist.

NOTE

It is the author's intention that the play be performed in three acts: Overture/Module 1; Module 2; Module 3/Coda.

KEY

...   A breath (not a pause) between words and thought.

—   Thoughts arriving faster than words; an abrupt interruption.

ΩΩ   Bacchantes; the ritualistic possession of a single character or characters; a heightened or subtle change of reality distinguishable in the gradual distortion of environment and behavior; an approaching storm.

Ω   A return to normalcy; recovery from a drunkard state; sudden reawakening or sad recognition.

≈   Overlapping of dialogue, argumentative; rapid and/or symphonic speech.

ANTHESTERIA   Opening of new wine at the festival for Dionysus.

BROMIOS   The roar of thunder.

COMPOSITIO MEMBRORUM   The piecing together of limbs. (See the Byzantine play, *The Passion of Christ*, in which Agave, mother of Pentheus, fits the severed head of her son onto the remainder of his corpse. Also see the introduction to *Bakkhai* by Reginald Gibbons and Charles Segal, Oxford University Press, New York, 2001.)

DEUS EX MACHINA The expulsion of all artificial contrivance (or *mechane*); the beginning of comprehension; a divine intervention wherein a god, authoritative figure or epiphany appears to solve the insoluble, explaining all mysteries of plot and circumstance; god from the machine.

DITHYRAMB Solemn odes and hymns sung to Dionysus at festivals, or chant relating some incident in the life of the god to whom it is addressed; wild ecstatic hymn of texts; a tragic literary form; the act of delivering a formal speech to an audience, slowly building to a frenzied, impassioned choral poetic expression, not unlike a sermon or chanted prayer.

HUBRIS Sudden outbreak.

OREIBASIA Religious procession of ritualistic walking toward mountainous regions.

SPARAGMOS Ritualistic rending of the body.

GLOSSARY

BALDRIC A belt worn over one shoulder, crossing the chest diagonally, used to support weapons or musical instruments.

CHITONISKOS A short tunic.

CUIRASS A breastplate.

PEPLOS Garment of wool, linen or silk draped from shoulder to ankle, held together by pins or brooches.

SAKKOS A hairnet.

THYRSUS A sword.

O V E R T U R E

Remembering the Act of Forgetting

The training and education we were giving them was all a dream, and they only imagined all this was happening to them and around them; but in truth they were being molded and trained down inside the earth, where they and their arms and all their trappings were being fashioned. When they were completely made, the earth their mother delivered them from her womb; and now they must take thought for the land in which they live, as for their mother and nurse, must plan for her and protect her, if anyone attacks her, and they must think of the other citizens as brothers also born from the earth.

—PLATO
THE REPUBLIC, BOOK III

The Museum of Antiquities possesses the characteristic objects of an older period in a world long past—an eternal history reawakening—something reminiscent of an ancient meeting room in ruin. Its corridors, where romantic and classical paintings once hung, are empty. An indefinable nostalgic past blurs and softens the lines of a contemporary world just beyond its doors. There is only the faint light of darkness bleeding through the broken leaded glass of heroic-sized windows, casting sharp and angular shapes onto an endless floor of Venetian marble (where the marble tiles are cracked or missing, blue earth is revealed). A massive chandelier, barely lit and hanging from the center of an intricately carved rosette, introduces a painted mural on the ceiling. At every turn there are statues, and vases—some broken, some in tact—resting on pedestals or propped against a wall. In the middle of this great hall stands an ancient stone catafalque draped in stark white linen and iridescent silks embroidered with gold. It is set like a banquet table. A blinding light is cast down onto the surface of the table, crowded with baskets of fruit, nuts, platters of bread and cheese, flasks of olive oil, silver pitchers of water and wine, vessels of cut glass, and alabaster urns. The *surrounding area is littered with stacks of leather-bound books, film reels, album jackets and typewritten manuscripts with notes inked across their pages. Four sturdy chairs are placed behind the banquet table, and two chairs (much more elaborate) are set at each end. Microphones are set before each chair. Downstage of the table, a podium. Upstage, a balcony at the top of a marble staircase.*

Ω Ω

Music: intrepid violin, cello, harp.

The five panelists—Ion, Meno, Phaedo, Crito, Apollodoros— are in profile outside the window. A beleaguered figure, the Moderator, is slumped over at the bottom of the stairs with an open book balanced in his lap. Apollodoros, descends from the balcony carrying an alabaster bust (the head of Pentheus) under her arm. She is striking, with sharp eyes set in sculpted copper. She is aware of the young man, but she does not acknowledge him. Apollodoros surveys the room . . . pausing only to distinguish one object from the other; runs her fingers along the surface of the walls, presses her ear to the ground, listens . . . counts the figures on the ceiling above her, takes in air. She deposits her bust on an empty pedestal, delivers her face to the audience, smiles, lifts one of the vases high above her head.

APOLLODOROS: Exhibit A: Large-belly amphora displaying an exquisitely drawn warrior dressed in a diaphanous chitoniskos beneath an elaborately decorated cuirass. Warrior against tradition. He stands looking off pensively to the right. In his left hand—a thyrsus. His right hand is propped on his hip. A cloak is draped over one arm, a sword hangs from a baldric that crosses his chest . . . *(Holding the second vase against her hip)* Exhibit B: Red female figure. She wears a crown of figs on her head, a peplos and sakkos, holds a vessel for libation, plays the instruments of self possession . . . a lute . . . a lyre. She faces left. In turning the vase, one imagines direct contact between the woman on one side and the young man on the opposite side of the vase. The profiles of eyes on both figures are elaborate renditions. These vessels are empty. The eyes follow you as you go. *(Walking toward the audience)* Exhibit C: It has been said that one Sir Norman Victor, the man who built this house . . . these walls . . . it has been said he had an affair with one of his maidservants: a Negro girl. She was from the South. From *there*—somewhere *rural* and unrefined . . . She had a child. Shortly after the child was born, the girl vanished, left the child here . . . in this house . . . beneath this vaulted ceiling . . . never returned. The boy was raised by the servants . . . slept beneath the god of tradition—looking to his mother to return to him one day. *(Kneeling beside the Moderator, whispering in his ear)* Exhibit D: An unidentified woman lies amongst the ruins on a marble floor. Victim is female. The deceased is a woman of an indeterminate age . . . of average height and body weight . . . simple cotton A-lined dress of maximum length. No shoes . . . no jewelry . . . no visible scars . . . no identification. No family has claimed the body. *(Gently placing her finger tips to his brow, spine, heart and skull)* Cause of death: crushed skull, broken vertebrae, shattered breastplate, piercing left lung. Contusions to cranium. Abrasions to spinal column. Death by fall.

Ω

(The Moderator quakes into awakening. Apollodoros has seated herself at the table. The Moderator embarks upon the tedious journey toward the podium where he comes to rest his book . . . He looks out into the audience, returns

his attention to his book, flips through its pages, hesitates, proceeds with some trepidation. Procession of the panel.)

OREIBASIA

THE MODERATOR:
>His mother saw that his hair was black. All of it. He had all of his hair and all of it—black. All the hair he would ever have he already had . . . He came with it . . . thick and black and dark . . . Enough hair for all the world . . . Dark. Darker than black, all of it . . . And she saw that he had all of his fingers too, and all of his toes . . . each one of them . . . And a penis and scrotum and eyes for seeing already focused on her . . . And already his eyes were distracted to see something else beyond her . . . something unfamiliar . . . Already something had ended as quickly as it had begun . . . And already she missed him and sobbed at the great distance between them as he lay on her breast, new and growing old and covered in blood . . . New with all of his hair . . . black . . . All the hair he could ever have he already had and already he had finished drinking from her, was full and contented and fell to sleep again . . . Already satisfied . . . wanting nothing else from her for now . . . wanting nothing else except to retreat into himself and the privacy of sleep . . . Already he could do that for himself . . . He had all of his hair and all of his toes . . . There was nothing more she could give him for now . . . For now . . . nothing else he needed . . . Except to sleep . . . And already he could do that for himself . . . And already she pained at the great distance between their lives.

(He closes the book, leaves the podium and addresses the audience through the darkness:)

Welcome—to regression. Here . . . where we are now— in the cancellation of time and space—where music plays, and some teach and some learn and others argue the relevance of this . . . the relevance of here . . . I am trying to stay here, where I am . . . but I am retreating backward. We are not taught to retreat. We are taught to advance. To walk forward—from the place of our beginning . . . which makes me all the more curious about the ground behind us. The ground we have not covered . . . They were . . . forgotten, you see. Forgotten words . . . hidden away in some obscure library . . . incarcerated words trapped in the damp basement archives of some university's library . . . pieces of him, waiting . . . unstirred . . . words . . . discovered by me— an unimportant man of unimportant letters . . . the youngest of my colleagues—the least accomplished except that I found him, and invited you all here to know him. To know his words as I found them decomposing in that crypt. I pulled them up with delicate force—like exhuming fossils embedded in rock . . . carefully brought them back to you—who had forgotten. Now you have them again . . . you see, upon first reading *Mother and Son*, a novel by Archer Aymes—upon first seeing the cracking leather spine of it barely clothed beneath a tattered book jacket—azure blue paper framing a silver gelatin print of a woman and a boy, their faces obscured by sepia shadows. Upon first reading those words printed on fraying paper: "His mother saw that his hair was black. All of it," I was . . . transformed . . . returned to ignorance.

(An attempted explanation) When I discovered it, I felt like I . . . like I had written it . . . I was . . . compelled . . . to organize this conference . . . in celebration of this unusual book . . . to commemorate this unusual—it's the only published book by this writer—curiously short for a novel, there are only one hundred and forty pages . . . yet so completely dense and bewildering, the style of it even

ii
... not unlike Gabriel García Márquez's *Leaf Storm*, published just four years prior, short, dense and lyrical. And I wondered if, like me, Archer Aymes had read *Leaf Storm*. I wonder if he'd come upon it, and like me ... sat on a barstool smoking two packs of cigarettes ... reading the words out loud to himself over countless glasses of gin and lime ... I wondered how his body was positioned when he read it ... if he read it ... wondered if Aymes read Márquez the way I read Aymes ... if he thought to himself, that he must respond ... to ... "memory, myth and the nature of time bursting into

iii
lovely shameless blossoms ..."

(A sentimental pause, then catches himself) The vortex from which Márquez chooses to tell his story—to view the world—keeps changing, as it does in Aymes's *Mother and Son*. The scene may remain the same, but the narrative is never the same—the landscape is never the same—and as soon as it is described, as soon as something has been said, it's said again. Except what was said before is not exactly what is being said now, and that makes what was said before already forgotten, already something *nostalgic* ... living in our memory.

(Introspective, gaining confidence) How can we know what is to be said next? What would Aymes say now? What would he say about the earth if he had inhabited it longer? For I believe that is who the mother is—the earth—and the son is the artist, *born* of the earth, with eyes to see—

(Too loud, too confident) And those who dismiss this as poetry—those who embrace it simply as a story of a mother and a son—miss the point of it, I think. He said ... *(Slows down)* He said there would be no more art ... he said that ... yet here we are ... we are here ... I am here ... looking at some art ... trying to see it ...

(A private moment) Speculation . . . belief . . . redemption . . . revision . . . we're moving *toward* . . .

closer to . . . a *new beginning* . . . moving as if there had been an *old beginning* that failed us. Some of us will never admit to witnessing an ending . . . some of us . . . we move on denying there has been an ending of any kind because the word itself—an *ending*—is too . . . uh . . . well, final, I suppose. Conjures something religious and dreaded in our collective conscious . . . an apocalyptic insanity . . . anti-intellectual to speak of an ending of space and a cancellation of history . . . and yet, for some of us . . . it is our defense . . . to agree . . . on an ending— the ending of an era . . . of fresh food in the market place . . . of love . . . of God. It comforts us to think we were once privy to something else . . . that is no more . . . for this reason—we access eras long gone . . . summon those who carry memory in their back pockets— because maybe . . . just maybe . . . there is a chance—for the revival of some old idea . . . an opportunity for a . . . continuum.

(*To someone in the audience*) Suppose . . . suppose you had been told that—you were convinced to *believe* that you were at your beginning . . . convinced to believe that *your* beginning was *the* relevant marker of time . . . And you believed there had been many wonderful things—*beginnings*—before you . . . magnificent inventions—the evidence all around you, in the magnitude of great city ruins, and the booty of lost treasures, the fragments of recorded genius—and all of this was waiting for you—you!—to reach back, to take from it what was valuable and timeless—an inheritance to bring into the room of your beginnings—and then . . . someone told you your inheritance had lost its value. The last inventor's idea was already irrelevant before he had fully realized it. The design of it was predicated upon invention in an era of demolition. And you—a generation removed from the end of all things—have nothing to inherit except . . . useless tools manufactured for outdated machines . . . you are not at the beginning . . . you've arrived at the ending . . .

(*Returns to podium*) As many of you . . . uh . . . know, this conference has already met with some—controversy. I am here now, as your moderator. I will do my best to honor that vocation. There are many to thank for their contribution to this conference and we will attempt to do that later but there is so much planned. I am proud to have invited these that know—to engage in the process toward knowing. I have been told that most of what I think I know is incorrect. Today I will try to forget what I think I know . . . so that, hopefully, we can move beyond just a critical disagreement regarding a man's aesthetic value . . . and move *on* . . . to something . . . more.

(*Lights up on the panelists positioned at the table.*)

iv   I introduce my esteemed guests—Ion: journalist, editor, translator of poetry, literary critic, biographer and, at present, completing what promises to be the first—

ION: The definitive—

v   THE MODERATOR: —biography of Archer Aymes. Phaedo: filmmaker, film historian, formerly a student and artistic collaborator of Aymes and, of course, principle actress

vi   in his film, *Mother and Son*. Meno: celebrated radio and television personality and the only American talk show host to have interviewed Aymes during his life. And,

vii   last but not least, I'm honored to introduce Crito: civil rights activist, internationally renowned musician, recording artist of more than twenty albums, his first album being *Mother and Son, Volume I*, released in 1974, based on his last encounter with Aymes on the Mule Train March in 1968—

CRITO: Don't expect—I mean, I'm sayin'—don't ya'll look for too much from me this time around. I'm too fucked-up about some of this shit. I may get there, I may not. I mean, I just left Wayne Shorter and Freddie Hubbard lying in the street so there ain't too much else I got to say about this other than what I already said.

THE MODERATOR: Oh—I almost forgot—A-Apollo-pollodoros— viii she unexpectedly joins us today. I . . . I have no formal biography of—

APOLLODOROS: Performance artist. Gossip monger. Gate-keeper. Truth purveyor. Barfly. Bitch.

THE MODERATOR: I welcome . . . all of you . . . into this curious room of forgetting what had been remembered.

M O D U L E 1

The Myth of Tomorrow:
A Technical Discourse on Mutation

Since art is informed by something beyond its power,
all we could successfully enact was a dance of doubt.
—DEREK WALCOTT

Becoming cannot be a given . . . if already I am no
longer what I was, it is still necessary that I have to
be so in the unity of a nihilating syhnthesis which
I sustain in (my) being; otherwise I would have no
relation of any sort with what I am no longer . . .
—JEAN-PAUL SARTRE

It's not easy to trace the development of one's own
sensibility. One can readily see what one has *become*,
which events have shaped the course of one's life.
But what always stays out of reach, remains more
or less concealed, is precisely what might have cat-
alyzed these events, the something . . .
—ANDRÉ BRETON

What others want you to be you are going to be,
despite all evidence to the contrary. —GORE VIDAL

On what lines will you look, Socrates, for a thing
of whose Nature you know nothing at all? —MENO

Apollodoros opens the first bottle of wine.

ANTHESTERIA

(The Moderator is seated at the head of table, facing the panel.)

PHAEDO: How shall we begin?

THE MODERATOR *(Flipping through color-coded index cards)*: I'd like to begin with Meno. You were the first to—

MENO: Introduce Aymes to America—

ION *(Sharply)*: We should begin—

MENO: Just like Ed Sullivan introduced Elvis and The Beatles. **ix** Ed made Presley sing to a slobbering hound dog . . . great show. You see I came from the—

ION *(Cutting him off)*: —We will begin as we agreed to begin!

(Lights dim on the panel. Ion proceeds to the podium and reads from a manuscript, for the audience.)

(Soberly) Taken from the *Village Voice*, dated January 8th, 1970: ARCHER AYMES: WRITER, FILMMAKER, DEAD AT THE AGE OF FORTY.

PHAEDO: Thirty-four—he was thirty-four!

ION:

Archer Aymes, a controversial figure as well known for his 1959 award-winning experimental novel, *Mother and Son* as for his mercurial and offbeat cynicism, was found dead in his jail cell on the morning of January 1st in a New York State penitentiary where he had been awaiting trial for unlawful protest and second-degree manslaughter. Police and prison officials have ruled the cause of Mr. Aymes's death as being an apparent suicide.

PHAEDO: It was NOT apparent!

ION:

Born in Marks, Mississippi, Archer Aymes attended Columbia College. In 1959, while a senior student at Columbia College, his first novel, *Mother and Son* was published, briefly catapulting Mr. Aymes to what some critics called undeserved celebrity status. An uncomfortable figure in the literary vanguard, Archer Aymes eventually withdrew from the limelight as quickly as he'd entered it, and, as predicted by early skeptics, never published again. From 1962 to 1968, Archer Aymes taught experimental fiction at New York University. During this time Mr. Aymes formed the short-lived Dionysus Arts & Film Center. There, with the assistance of a small group of film students, he wrote, produced and directed *Mother And Son*, a silent impressionistic short film based on his then out-of-print novel. Sometime shortly thereafter, Archer Aymes abruptly resigned from his position at New York University. In 1969, Mr. Aymes's film, *Mother and*

Son, was awarded The Bunuel Prize at The Tenth Annual New York Avant-Garde Film Festival, but failed to receive national distribution or critical validation.

PHAEDO: Ha!

ION:

In October of 1970, Mr. Aymes organized a protest at The Museum of Antiquities in New York City . . .

APOLLODOROS *(Under, for all to hear)*: A poetic, moral, political revolt, resisting all things derived from all things of a . . . cortical understanding.

ION:

. . . espousing his doomsday ideology of "The End of Art and the Revolution of the Poor." The two-hour demonstration spawned a riot between police, and some twenty-five Aymes postulants, resulting in the accidental death of an as-yet-unidentified woman—believed to be an innocent bystander. During his internment, Mr. Aymes declined interviews with the press, embarking upon a self-imposed silence.

(He closes his manuscript.)

Archer Aymes left behind no known relatives. No plans for the body had been made.

APOLLODOROS: There was no body. There is no body.

(Beat. Lights up on the table.)

THE MODERATOR: Meno, on your television show in the fall of 1959—

MENO: Fourth season—

THE MODERATOR: Yes . . .

MENO: Nine seasons in all—did you know I also produced for
x television? *The Subject Is Jazz*, with Gilbert Seldes, in
kinescope—

THE MODERATOR: I didn't know that, but—

MENO: Few others on television doing what I was doing at
that time.

THE MODERATOR: What I'd like to get to—

MENO: Oh, you had Milton Berle's *Texaco Theater*—

THE MODERATOR: is—

MENO: Mike Wallace on CBS, John Wingate on *Nightbeat*—

THE MODERATOR: Archer Aymes—

MENO: And the king, of course—my good friend—

THE MODERATOR: I'd like to ask you about—

xi MENO: Steve Allen! We had a friendly competition thing
going—learned a lot from Allen. Like Steve Allen I'd
come from radio—played jazz and race records on
radio. Oh, this is *waay* before *you* were born—

THE MODERATOR: But when you—

MENO: Introduced Ruth Brown and Little Richard to America—told jokes between records—that's what made *my*
Little Richard all the more palatable to America—

THE MODERATOR: I read that. Now—let's focus down. 1959, you
and—

THE MODERATOR AND MENO: Aymes—

MENO: None of that footage exists, everything from '55 to
'59—LOST. We were *live* in those days.

THE MODERATOR: So, the interview was—

MENO *(Wink and a smile)*: No different from the rest.

APOLLODOROS: Next question!

*(Apollodoros gets up from the table, pours herself a glass of
wine . . . pays careful attention.)*

THE MODERATOR: Was Aymes the only guest on your show, or—

MENO: What're you kidding? *Oh noooo!* Had to have a *REEAAL* celebrity as your feature in those days—

APOLLODOROS *(Sarcastically)*: Eddie Fisher.

MENO: A matinee idol or a movie starlet or something—

PHAEDO: Rock Hudson, Dagmar.

MENO: Eye candy. Then you'd introduce your filler midway through—intellectual types, politicians, writers—

PHAEDO: Animal trainers, etc.

MENO: Then I'd wake everybody up with a couple of jokes, a skit or a song—

APOLLODOROS *(Mock singing)*: "Ooh Poppa Doo!"

MENO: Sign off with: "From me to you, keep it red, keep it white, keep it blue . . ."

MENO AND APOLLODOROS: "Good night, America!"

APOLLODOROS *(An offering to the others)*: Cheese?

THE MODERATOR: What did you and Aymes talk about on your—

MENO: Oh, he said he was born in Clarks, Mississippi—

THE MODERATOR: Marks—Marks Mississippi.

MENO: Said his mother was a Russian Jewish immigrant—

APOLLODOROS: Greek.

MENO: Who came to the U.S. from—

THE MODERATOR: Greece.

MENO: His father was a Negro . . . didn't stick around—

ION: He knew little of his father—

MENO: Except that he was apparently a Negro.

THE MODERATOR: Apparently.

MENO: And his mother died shortly after he was born.

PHAEDO: He was twelve!

MENO: Like I said, shortly after he was born—he was twelve or so—his mother died.

THE MODERATOR: So, when you first met Aymes—

MENO: When I first met Aymes, in 1950, he was—

THE MODERATOR: Nine—

MENO: What?

THE MODERATOR: You said when you *first met Aymes in 1950*—

xii

APOLLODOROS: Peacetime!

THE MODERATOR: I'm assuming you meant *1959*.

MENO: When I first *interviewed* Aymes it was 1959. He was . . . thirty or so—

THE MODERATOR: Twenty-three.

MENO: Whatever—but when I first met Aymes it was in 1950. See, Kerouac had a friend named Bill Cannastra, lived down on 21st Street—died rather tragically on the subway—

PHAEDO: Drunk.

xiii ION: Ginsberg wrote about it in *Howl*.

xiv MENO: Everybody would go to Cannastra's—especially all the writers. I knew all the writers in my day—didn't read 'em all, but I knew 'em all. I was fascinated with writers—the way they talked. Didn't know what the hell they were talkin' about, but I was fascinated. I knew Tennessee Williams—Cannastra and Williams had been, shall we say, *involved*? I knew Gore Vidal—

APOLLODOROS: Living.

MENO: When he was hanging out with Anais Nin—

APOLLODOROS: Dead.

MENO: trying to help out Jimmy Baldwin.

APOLLODOROS: Dead.

MENO: Jack Kerouac—

APOLLODOROS: Still dead.

MENO: he used to hang out at The West End Bar where I used to hang out.

xv ION: Van Doren introduced Kerouac to Giroux who had also gone to Columbia.

MENO: As had Kerouac—all good drinking buddies of mine for a time.

THE MODERATOR: But WHAT does this have to do with Archer Aymes?

MENO: Aren't we talking about when I first *met* Archer Aymes?

THE MODERATOR: Well, that's what I'm trying to get to.

MENO: Well, that's what I'm trying to tell you!

THE MODERATOR: Well, Aymes was only twenty-three when you interviewed him in '59—

ION: Or so he claimed.

THE MODERATOR: In 1950 he would've only been about fourteen years old—

MENO: Fourteen? No, he was *muuuuch* older than that! At least eighteen! You *had* to be at Cannastra's parties!

THE MODERATOR: Are you sure about—

MENO *(Stridently)*: I remember him being there—a nobody then—Vidal asked me who he was. I didn't know. I don't think anybody knew—he was just standing there . . . with this nervous, tortured look . . . like Montgomery Clift, but more arrogant.

APOLLODOROS *(Second offering to the others)*: Figs?

MENO: Vidal said he thought he was beautiful—an apparition. **xvi** Wondered where he was from . . . you know, what country, because his features were so unusual.

THE MODERATOR: Unusual how?

APOLLODOROS: Black!

MENO: No . . . no . . . he was very fair . . .

PHAEDO: Cerulean.

MENO: I thought he was Puerto Rican—

THE MODERATOR: Why a Puerto Rican?—

MENO: The Puerto Ricans had just started coming to New York at that time. Lived over where Lincoln Center is **xvii** now—real slum in those days—you know, *West Side Story*. What's with the face?

THE MODERATOR: I'm sorry but I'm having a hard time with this . . . *(Holding up a card)* See? Red card—timeline—

APOLLODOROS *(To the Moderator)*: Bet you went to college and all, huh?

THE MODERATOR: Aymes enrolled as an undergraduate at Columbia at the age of twenty in 1956.

MENO: I don't care when he enrolled at Columbia! CANNAS-TRA WAS DEAD BY 1950—decapitated on the train as I told you!

(Uncomfortable beat.)

THE MODERATOR: I'm listening.

(Apollodoros pours Meno a glass of water. He pops a pill.)

xviii MENO: Pollack was there—he remembers Aymes from that night, ask him—

APOLLODOROS: Dead. Still dead.

MENO: Vidal noticed him first . . . he was standing there . . . watching everybody . . . like he was studying us—and Vidal suggested we study him . . . made a little game of it . . . and at some point . . . all of us, were just standing there . . .

(Apollodoros sets a martini glass in Meno's hand.)

ΩΩ

Ice melting in our glasses . . . fixated on him . . . he was good looking . . . very good looking . . . athletic build—

PHAEDO: Slight.

MENO: Standing by a window, rolling a cigarette . . . mess of curly black hair, unruly. Clear complexion—

APOLLODOROS *(An offering to Meno)*: Olive?

MENO: Wet . . . his face was very wet . . . shiny like glass. Beardless. He was wearing these tweed trousers . . . wool . . . creased . . . this white cotton shirt buttoned up to the neck . . . hot that night . . . all the windows open . . . fans going—no air—sleeves were rolled up . . . worker's arms . . . veins running through . . . But he

28

never, he never unbuttoned that shirt . . . and his shoes, I think I noticed his shoes first because they were an old style—black wing tips, like my father used to wear— but Aymes's were worn down . . . split . . . too big for him . . . but they'd been shined . . . he looked like an immigrant who'd just wandered into a foreign country.

THE MODERATOR: Did he say anything?

(Apollodoros lights a cigarette, places it between Meno's fingers.)

MENO: Lit his cigarette . . . craned his neck toward the window . . . arrogant little smile . . . he knew we were watching him.

THE MODERATOR: Did you talk to him at all?

Ω

APOLLODOROS *(Out of nowhere, to the Moderator)*: Oooh, you gots a whole *mess* a questions, you do!

MENO: Of course I talked to him! That's what I DO—walked right over to him. Thinking he was a Puerto Rican I introduced myself in Spanish, you know, *bueno noches, me llamo* blah blah, that sort of thing. Boy was I shocked when he opened his mouth!

THE MODERATOR: Why was that?

MENO: Veeery well spoken. Too well spoken. "I don't come here REG-YU-LAR-LEE," he said . . . that kind of thing. Here I'm thinkin' this kid is a 'Rican!

PHAEDO: And when he told you he was black?

MENO: He didn't say anything about being black.

ION: Interesting. Make note, address later . . .

APOLLODOROS: The man didn't have to say he was black!

THE MODERATOR: So Meno, what else did the two of you talk about that night?

MENO: Oh for God's sake—it was fifty years ago, how am I supposed to remember what the hell else we—

PHAEDO: So let's move on—

MENO: He said he was taking some classes over at The New School, I told him I was in radio, and I think I pointed out to him who was who, did he know so and so, etc. He cut me off, said he already knew who was who . . . wasn't impressed with any of us, didn't care about all these "so-called writers . . . entertainers," he called us. Said he had no artistic aspirations at all. "Trapped"—all of us, he said.

THE MODERATOR: You must've been very offended.

MENO: He was fascinated with everybody in the room, including me! I knew that much—I knew what *he* was, before he knew what he was.

THE MODERATOR: What's that?

PHAEDO: Talented!

MENO: And *afraid* of *being* talented . . .

THE MODERATOR: I don't follow you.

MENO *(Directed at the Moderator)*: Young . . . smart . . . knew everything before he knew anything . . . you know the type. Anyway, I don't remember much else—I was a heavy drinker in those days—everybody was—this is before recovery became so damned fashionable. —Oh! Somebody threw up all over his shoes. *(Laughing)* I remember that!

PHAEDO *(Dryly)*: Of course you do.

MENO: I brought the whole thing up to him, about that night at Cannastra's, the very next time I saw him.

THE MODERATOR: And when was this?

MENO: March of '59—a book party—I don't remember for whom but Kerouac's *Dharma Bums* had just come out. Vidal was there, Ginsberg, I don't remember who else. —Oh! Boris Pasternak was there—*Doctor Zhivago*!

xix PHAEDO: Pasternak wasn't even *in* the United States—EVER!

MENO: Tibor de Nagy Gallery—Upper East Side—very chic— xx
ION: John Bernard Myers. xxi
PHAEDO: No, no, it was *downtown* then—
ION: No, Upper East Side—
THE MODERATOR: John Bernard Myers?
MENO: Avant-garde fruit!
THE MODERATOR: I'm sorry, I don't know who—
APOLLODOROS: Keep up, baby! We playin' 4/4!
PHAEDO *(To the Moderator)*: Myers *made* painters like Alfred
    Leslie, Pollack, de Kooning—
MENO: Only if Clement Greenberg approved! xxii
ION: First to publish Frank O'Hara, John Ashbery—
MENO: Right, in *Semi-Colon*— xxiii
PHAEDO *(To the Moderator)*: Darling, are you published?
THE MODERATOR: Uh . . . no.

(Beat.)

PHAEDO: Well . . . no rush.
MENO: So, here we are, and I escorted Lara somebody or
    other, a model. Very thin, always wore black, drew her
    eyebrows on with charcoal. Wanted to be a Method
    actress—used to practice attempting suicide by jumping
    off the little bridge in Central Park. Wanted desperately
    to play Ophelia one day—the Method was very big at
    that time—anyway, Vladimir Nabokov was there, drink- xxiv
    ing up all the vodka, you know . . . *Lolita.*
THE MODERATOR: I had no idea Aymes knew Nabokov or—
PHAEDO: Darling, *nobody* knew Nabokov!
MENO: So there was Aymes, It had been about three months
    since they'd printed the excerpt of *Mother and Son* in . . .
    oh, uh—
ION: The *New Yorker.*
PHAEDO: No, no, no.

MENO: And so Lara somebody or other—she'd been carrying the *Mother and Son* story around in her handbag ever since it came out—she said the excerpt made her cry. She'd been using it in her Method classes. Said, "I must meet him, I simply must!" So I walked over to him, introduced myself, assuming he *knew* who I was—I was on TV by then. I didn't make the connection at first, but, well it was the eyes—"*reg-yu-lar-lee*"! And he had that same look on his face . . . everybody was whispering, so I mentioned we had met years before at Cannastra's—

THE MODERATOR: Did he remember that?

MENO: Said he didn't—said he'd never met me before. Never even watched television. I knew that game—very fashionable at that time to say you never watched television—

PHAEDO: Still is.

MENO: So I congratulated him on the story in the *New Yorker*—

PHAEDO: It was NOT in the *New Yorker*—

xxv ION *(Disproving her)*: Robert M. Coates wrote the introduc—

MENO: I'd heard Robert Giroux was thinking about publishing the novel at Harcourt and Brace—

ION: The book was published at—

ION AND PHAEDO: Random House!

MENO: So I told Aymes I knew Giroux quite well. Maybe I'd put a good word in for him. He said he didn't think that would be necessary. Still arrogant—

THE MODERATOR: Because he'd had one short story published in—

xxvi ION *(Simultaneously)*: The *New Yorker!*

xxvii PHAEDO *(Simultaneously)*: *Esquire!*

xxviii APOLLODOROS *(Simultaneously)*: *Black Tail!*

MENO: And because people had been seeing him around—having drinks with very important writers, such as Truman Capote.

PHAEDO: No, no—

MENO: Capote didn't drink with just anybody—he was very opportunistic and very paranoid.

THE MODERATOR: You would see him having drinks with Capote? You would run into them together?

PHAEDO: Capote was in MOSCOW in '59!

MENO: Oh, no, no, nothing like that. I'm sure wherever they went it was somewhere dangerous where young writers could feed on fodder for their literary souls! I was living on the Upper East Side at that time.

THE MODERATOR: Then how do you know he was hanging out with Capote?

MENO: Well . . . it had been rumored—

THE MODERATOR: So you're saying his celebrity was being created because of rumors—because of the *myths* of his associations?

MENO: Associations are very important! Everyone's interested in associations. Very interested! I'm always interested in a man's associations—how else do you know a person or judge his character? I even heard he was hanging out with the French writer—

ION: Jean Genet—

MENO: —who spoke quite highly of his short story in an interview.

THE MODERATOR: Genet?

PHAEDO: Genet was in jail in '59—

ION: Genet was very big on the abstract—

MENO: And *very* big on black people at that time—Genet had a very big abstract play all about *black* people on the Lower East Side at that time. I didn't understand a word of it—NOT A WORD OF IT—all that unintelligible symbolism and intellectual mumbo-jumbo . . . but that's what the kids were into. So Aymes was hot! Anyway, Aymes and I are standing there, everybody's looking at us, inching closer to see if they can hear what we're talking about—so I brought up Capote and Genet—

THE MODERATOR: *Associations* . . .

MENO: I asked him if he had many writers as friends—

MENO AND THE MODERATOR: "No such thing, writers who are friends . . ."

(Meno is somewhat stunned by the Moderator quoting Aymes.)

ION: Henry Miller also spoke quite highly of Aymes's book—

THE MODERATOR: Miller spoke of Aymes?

MENO: Yeah, but did you read what Herbert Gold said in the *Nation*? "Another piece of crap!" I had that one tacked to Aymes's dressing-room wall the night he was on my show. Gold always did have a sense of humor. Aymes didn't. Gold *haaaaated* Kerouac, and *haaaated* all those Kerouacian knockoffs!

THE MODERATOR: You're saying that's all Aymes was—a knock-off of Jack Kerouac?

MENO: So, anyway . . . we're talking, and next thing I know there's a little halo of cigarettes and martinis all around us—we've got an audience, see. And so I said, "Well, Archer, tell me, do you see yourself as belonging to a group of peers with whom you share a similar aesthetic or social outlook?" And he said—

MENO AND THE MODERATOR: "No."

MENO *(Again, taken aback)*: Yes . . . dry . . . very dry . . . just like that . . . and the little halo chuckled . . . I mean, you'd think I'd intentionally *insulted* him.

THE MODERATOR: Had you?

MENO: No . . . no . . . I mean . . . I thought all writers were part of a generation—especially at that time! But he was insistent on not being associated with anybody—the Beats—anybody.

THE MODERATOR: Why do you think that was?

MENO: He said America hadn't produced any real models for people like him—not even black people! Well, I didn't know what he meant by that!

ION *(Laughing)*: Because you didn't know he was black.

MENO: Who knew? So I was about to give him my card, invite him out for drinks, but he excused himself and pushed through the crowd. Walked right out. One of the rudest people I ever—

THE MODERATOR: That's not the image I have of—the man who wrote this book. I mean—was he really that—

PHAEDO *(Over him)*: We should talk about the film—examine that body of work, examine *that* body!

THE MODERATOR: I need to—I would like—would just like to— I need to go back—to track this—

APOLLODOROS *(To the Moderator)*: Take. Your. Time!

(Beat.)

THE MODERATOR: Okay . . . *(Muddles through his index cards)* While Aymes was at Columbia . . . he pursued and cultivated his interest in literature . . . and according to an interview he gave . . . just before the fall of his junior year—

PHAEDO: 1958.

THE MODERATOR: —he wrote *Mother and Son.*

PHAEDO: The first thing he had ever written—

THE MODERATOR: —and the first day of the fall semester, Aymes gave his only copy of it to an English composition professor, asked if he would read it and talk to him about it. And a couple of months later, after Aymes continuously pressured him for a response or at least the return of his manuscript, the English professor told Aymes not only did he not like what Aymes had written, he called the writing: "Nothing more than obscure unordered symbols and metaphors, void of plot or even poetic significance," told Aymes—

ION: "Privately charged symbols have meaning only to the writer"—

THE MODERATOR: Said Aymes should "forget about writing fiction until he's actually read some . . ."

MENO: Sounds about right.

THE MODERATOR: Aymes actually dropped out of school after that.

PHAEDO: He completed his studies a year later.

ION: But Mark Van Doren—

MENO *(Driving his point)*: Who knew Aymes from the hanging-out at Bill Cannastra's and The West End Bar in the early '50s—

THE MODERATOR: Van Doren accidentally came upon the copy of Aymes's manuscript on the English professor's desk, and he read it, right?

ION: Right.

THE MODERATOR: Was so impressed with it he sent it toooo . . .

MENO: Robert Giroux—

THE MODERATOR: Who was also impressed with it, and he submitted it to—

ION: Robert M. Coates at the *New Yorker*—

PHAEDO: No. No. No. Clay Felker published it at *Esquire*. Joe Fox published it at Random House!

MENO: And the *New Yorker* decided to run the excerpt in February of '59—

ION: Ten pages or so.

PHAEDO: No. No. No.

MENO: Giroux knew what he was doing.

THE MODERATOR: What was he doing?

ION: The *New Yorker* had never published anything that unconventional before.

MENO: I know. I subscribed. As soon as the story came out, the buzz started, see? You had the hipsters, like Ginsberg and Paul Goodman—

ION: Frank O'Hara—

MENO: The whole Cedar's Tavern crowd—

ION: Abstract Expressionists—

MENO: All those kids from 10th Street who thought Hofmann, Greenberg and Franz Kline were the holy trinity—

ION: They wrote into the *New Yorker*, praising the story—

THE MODERATOR: Right—

PHAEDO: Wrong!

THE MODERATOR *(Reaches for another card)*: Well somebody wrote in somewhere saying Aymes was doing:

> Something new with language, something you can only learn to read after you've killed that chamber in your brain that has already learned to read.

PHAEDO: Leonard Lymes—*New York Post*.

MENO: Yeah, well you also had the more scholarly types writing in, saying the *New Yorker* had reached an all time low—

PHAEDO: IT WAS NOT IN THE *NEW YORKER*!

ION: After the excerpt of *Mother and Son* was published, I interviewed Kenneth Rexroth for the *Village Voice*. *(Presumptuous acknowledgment of applause)* Thank you. And I asked him if he'd read the short story by a little known Columbia student named Archer Aymes—

MENO: And Rexroth said he read it, knew about the squabble—

ION: But thought it was all a scheme—

MENO: That Giroux had cooked up! The next new thing—

THE MODERATOR: —and Rexroth said the Beat Generation had turned into a "Madison Avenue gimmick," right?

MENO: And he was right—a GREAT gimmick!

THE MODERATOR: He also said Aymes's story was *not great*— why? I thought Rexroth would've been one of the *few* people who—

ION: He thought Aymes unsuccessfully attempted what he and Ferlinghetti began—jazz poetry.

MENO: And who cares?

THE MODERATOR: So, is that when Seymour Krim wrote his response to Rexroth in the *Voice*—

ION: Suggesting that modern writers, like Aymes, wanted to—

THE MODERATOR: Get "deeper into reality than their predecessors"—

ION: To which Michael Harrington responded in a letter the very next week—

THE MODERATOR: Who was, who—

APOLLODOROS (*Like a monkey, mocking*): Who—who—who—was, who?

ION: Harrington said in his address to the Young Socialist League, "Whoever this young man is that everybody is talking about that wrote this little sentimental story about a boy and his mother, wrote nothing more than the chaotic amassing of detail." But he was really just taking a jab at Kerouac.

MENO: Kerouac was *famous*—Jack *knew* what he was doing—Aymes didn't!

PHAEDO: Kerouac had NOTHING to do with Aymes!

MENO: Kerouac had *everything* to do with *everybody* who was publishing for the first time in those days—everybody wanted the next Kerouac! Just like they had Marilyn Monroe but one Monroe is never enough—so you had Jayne Mansfield and Mamie Van Doren. Everybody loved Marilyn—everybody loved Kerouac!

ION: Not everybody.

PHAEDO: Not only did Kerouac NOT provide us with any answers, he never even raised the questions! Aymes did!

ION: Harrington said Kerouac had "yet to create a complex felt reality."

PHAEDO: *That* was the one thing he was *quite* correct about—his mistake was LUMPING AYMES WITH KEROUAC!

ION: Why are you yelling? I'm agreeing with you.

THE MODERATOR: So wasn't Harrington the one who said Aymes's story was just—

MENO: "Babble for babbling beatniks"—that was a good one!

PHAEDO: The great filmmaker, Maya Deren, also sent a letter **xxxiv** to the *Voice, sharply* disagreeing with Harrington!

THE MODERATOR: So why all the controversy?

MENO: Like he said . . . the story was . . . unconventional—

ION: Not the story as much as the *style* in which it was written—

THE MODERATOR: I understand that but what I'm asking is— even so—why did a ten-page short story create such a *huge* controversy among the, uh . . .

PHAEDO: Literati?

THE MODERATOR: Why was it so important?

ION: You see, there was a polar difference between the established modernists of the prewar generation and the new generation of postmodernist writers, who attempted to truly represent the antiacademic, antiestablishment— avant-garde . . .

THE MODERATOR: Yes, I understand that—

APOLLODOROS: You do? How very *magna cum laudey* of you!

ION: And at first glance, Aymes—just like the Beats—was a postmodernist . . .

PHAEDO: Postmodernism is architecture, not literature!

MENO: They were all just trying to be weird.

THE MODERATOR: So if he, Aymes, was just like the Beats, why was he singled out any more than—

ION: No! I never said Aymes was just *like* the Beats. I said he was *perceived* to be just like the Beats. And as for avant-gardism, David Lehman contends, and I would agree with him here: "If we are all postmodernists, we are none of us avant-garde, for postmodernism is the—"

ION AND THE MODERATOR: "institutionalization of the avant-garde."

ION: Aymes was more of an avant-gardist than a postmodernist—or at least he endeavored to be—

PHAEDO *(Over him)*: You're not answering the question. He asked you to explain—

ION: Excuse me, I'm trying to—

PHAEDO: He asked you *to explain* why the WORK—

ION: I'm trying to give him a context for—

PHAEDO: WHY THE WORK WAS IMPORTANT!!!

MENO: The Beats.

PHAEDO *(Standing)*: The Beats? The Beats! THE BEATS! I'm sick of this—the BEATS!

ION: Whether you're sick of it or not, he's right—the Beats at this time are connected to Aymes because they had been overexposed, were hugely popular and there was no other context for people to—

PHAEDO *(Over Ion, to the Moderator)*: AYMES CREATED! HE WAS A CREATIVE FORCE! NOT A MARKETING STRATEGY FOR THE BEATS! Aymes, in the book as well as in the film, dug deep—not only into his own subconscious, but into a universal subconscious— he struck a nerve in the universe and created a matrix of phantasmagoric complexes!

MENO: A what?

PHAEDO: He was a *real* artist who knew that *real life* retreated into dreams . . . he knew something more than so-called *realism* and THAT is the ONLY reason there was any controversy—

CRITO *(Leaning into the microphone)*: Because . . . postwar America . . . was obsessed . . . with postwar realism.

PHAEDO: Yes! He, like Maya Deren, created myths, invented divinities, and pondered for no practical purpose whatsoever on the nature of things—and in a time of true artlessness, a man made some art! That's why the work was IMPORTANT!

MENO: I don't think it was that important.

ION: May I? Recontextualization.

PHAEDO: *Ah mon dieu . . .*

XXXV

THE MODERATOR: I'm sorry?

ION: Recontextualization. The excerpt, the book was quite significant both because of the identity of Aymes, and what the book was supposed to be about: the sentimentality of its story, the relationship between a mother and her son—the maternal nature of this appealed to something people knew. It's classic—almost biblical—but because the novel is very avant-garde in style and structure, even more so than the novels of the Beats, it is automatically suspect of having a subversive message, possibly an unpatriotic coded manifesto against McCarthyism.

CRITO AND APOLLODOROS: Bullshit.

ION: The larger issue here is that Aymes's novel becomes much more significant than anything the Beats had written up to that point, because it was not like anything the Beats had written . . . it was much closer to surrealism. Aymes was recontextualizing . . . not unlike today's hip-hop.

CRITO: Ain't this a bitch—now he gonna break down hip-hop!

ION: Hip-hop, like jazz, was *born* in African-American urbanity!

APOLLODOROS: More wine?

PHAEDO: Yes!

CRITO: What?

ION: Hip-hop is the rebellious music of today, a new original American art form—

CRITO: I don't listen to that shit.

APOLLODOROS: They listen to you—

ION: But its popularity is reliant upon the act of sampling, and by taking these instrumental lines out of context and setting them in another context—taking what was old and putting it in something new—we are tricked into believing that what we are listening to is new, is different, but it's not. That's what Aymes's book did— *recontextualized*—tricked people—like today's Jay-Z.

MENO: Who?

CRITO: Ain't this some shit?

THE MODERATOR: Ion, if you don't mind, I think we should—

ION *(Adamant)*: Jay-Z used a line from the Broadway musical *Annie*—

CRITO: But what does this have to do with—

ION: Annie was the destitute orphan of America's land of opportunity—

MENO: In my day she was just a girl in the funny pages.

ION: In the Broadway musical of *Annie*, "Hard Knock Life," as sung by a chorus of little orphan girls, shows us the daily rigors of these defenseless girls who are forced to be laborers. But, when sampled by the rapper Jay-Z, the song becomes about *gangsta* life and *gangsta* ambitions.

(Ion stands, despite everyone's objection, begins an index-card recitation, very presentational:)

> I'm from the school of the hard knocks,
> We must not let outsiders violate our blocks,
> And my plot.
> Let's stick up the world and split it fifty-fifty,
> Uh-huh
> Let's take the dough and stay real jiggy,
> Uh-huh
> Let's sip the Cris and get pissy-pissy
> Flow imminently
> Like the memory of my nigga Biggie, baby!
> It's the hard knock life for us
> It's the hard knock life!!!

(Beat.)

. . . See?

(Ion returns to his seat.)

CRITO *(Seething, up-tempo)*: Recapitulation. Not no recontex- **xxxvi**
tualization, recapitulation—Beethoven, not no god-
damn cartoon Jay-Z bullshit. Beethoven—see—in classical music, you have the sonata form, a work in three or
four movements: exposition, development, recapitulation, based on a reconciliation of opposites. And in classical music, opposites are tonic versus dominate. Now,
the first theme in a classical sonata is tonic, the second
theme is dominant, and after the second theme, a development section. Each theme gets fragmented, extending
into far-reaching tonalities—some abstract shit. And
after the development section is the first theme as it was,
but the second theme which is in the dominant is now in
the tonic, which is a crucial turning point, because you
have to reroute *everything* back to the tonic—to the
point of RUPTURE. In the reconciliation period, you
have theme one: the tonic; and theme two: the dominant, but theme two is *now* the tonic. That's what Beethoven did—the true reconciliation of opposites—creating a coda, a fragment of a theme that had been done
earlier but now has its OWN life. And that's what
Aymes did—*SEE*?

(Beat.)

MENO: Yeah, so anyway, Aymes was *hot shit*—and Hentoff
capped the whole thing off by organizing a forum at the
92nd Street Y with uh . . . don't tell me—
ION: Norman Mailer, James Schuyler, Arthur Schlesinger . . .
PHAEDO: Lionel Trilling, Mary McCarthy . . .
ION: Norman Podhoretz.
MENO: Thank you.

THE MODERATOR: When was this?

ION: May of '59.

xxxvii APOLLODOROS *(Soft)*: Lady Day . . . live at the Phoenix . . .

MENO: I took Lara somebody or other—I don't know what-ever became of her—I think she eventually drowned herself or something . . .

APOLLODOROS: . . . Dying in Steve Allen's arms.

MENO: . . . Burroughs came with us. I'd just forgiven him for killing his wife—knew *her* quite well—lived on the Upper West Side back in the late '40s. She and her roommate used to have threesomes with Jack—

THE MODERATOR: So at the Y!

ION: Aymes was there.

MENO: Hentoff made sure of it.

THE MODERATOR: On the panel?

MENO: No—in the audience, because by then the argument between the old literature and the new was huge. And it all started from this kid's ten-page story in the *New Yorker*. Giroux had announced he was publishing Aymes's book in September, they'd put a rush on it, and word was out that Susskind had put an invitation out to Aymes to be on his show—I mean, Susskind never even invited Jack! Aymes was on his way to becoming the new golden boy of the Beat Generation, see?

THE MODERATOR: But I thought Aymes didn't consider himself a part of the Beat Generation—

xxxviii MENO: So anyway, Mailer and Schuyler really got into it, and Aymes is just sitting there, very quiet, arms folded, legs crossed, listening to them argue . . . waiting . . .

THE MODERATOR: For what?

xxxix MENO: Well, just like Hentoff planned, Schlesinger brought up the little story that ran in the *New Yorker*—the one everybody was talking about—

ION: He complained that the commercial market was all about the avant-garde, not creative writing—

MENO: "All these young writers may want to be rebels," he said, "but that's not what literature demands!"

THE MODERATOR: What does literature demand?

ION: A real social or political message people can use—

MENO: Right, that's what Schlesinger said, and somebody from the audience said art didn't have to be that—

CRITO: Art just has to be art!

MENO: Trilling chimed in and that got Schuyler yellin' at Schlesinger who's yellin' back about—

ION: The demise of American literature—

MENO: That got Mailer going, waving his fists around, you know how Mailer is, going on about—

ION: How American literature suffered from "bourgeois inverse snobbery," and the story he read in the *New Yorker* could've easily replaced the last twenty years of bullshit the American literary canon had put out—

MENO: That was it—applause, standing ovation! Aymes was in!

THE MODERATOR: What do you mean Aymes was *in?*

MENO: He could've had anything he wanted after that night. *Anything.*

APOLLODOROS *(From the stairs, looking up toward the balcony)*: But not everything!

THE MODERATOR: So what did Aymes do? Did he say anything?

MENO: He just sat there, while everybody stood up and screamed. And Mailer's challenging Schlesinger to a switchblade fight, and I look over to keep an eye on Aymes, but he's not in his seat anymore. I look around, he's slipping out the door, tryin' to sneak out unnoticed. So I run after him, wanted to get him on my show—

THE MODERATOR: Before Susskind or Allen got to him?

CRITO: You catchin' on.

MENO: He's headed to the subway, hands in his pockets, walking fast. I practically had to jog to catch up with him. And just before he got to the steps, I hooked him by the elbow, swung him around—the eyes, wide-open . . . wet like that night at Cannastra's—it finally hit him, he'd caught it by the tail, had it right in his hands, this thing he said he didn't want . . . this beautiful little stranger called celebrity . . . and he was in love with it, and he was scared to death!

APOLLODOROS *(From the stairs where she is now reclining)*: I know it ain't my turn . . . but what hasn't been said is that alla that shit about Aymes in 1950 is questionable, and what HASN'T been said is alla that shit about Aymes at The New School is *questionable*, and Aymes runnin' from ANYBODY is definitely QUESTIONABLE, and, what *hasn't* been said, is that before alla this, Columbia and the book and Norman Mailer with his switchblade, Aymes . . . well . . . *(Ghetto gossip downstage, to the audience)* The motherfucker was walkin' all ovuh the East Village back in the early to mid-'50s, doin' all kinds of things and *anybody* who was smokin' weed or playin' an instrument or havin' themselves a drink *anywhere* east of 4th Avenue and south of 14th Street could tell you that Aymes was hangin' out with that *white-freak poet* Maxwell Bodenheim—

MENO: Who?

APOLLODOROS: Who had found him a little young white girl to do all kinds a *freaky shit* with—

THE MODERATOR: Uh . . . Apollodoros, I think—

APOLLODOROS: And they would be hangin' out in them Greenwich Village bars lookin' for young men to go home with—'cause Bodenheim liked to *watch!*—

ION: Well, I—

APOLLODOROS: And so, some uh my friends, who will remain nameless, they will tell you that Aymes FUCKED Bodenheim's girlfriend somewhere in a flophouse ovuh on the Lower East Side—

PHAEDO: Exactly *who* are these friends of yours, dear?

xl

APOLLODOROS: And THAT'S where Aymes really got his first notions that he could write poetry, see—not from no college professors or publishers—but from *Bodenheim*. 'Cause Aymes would be FUCKIN' Bodenheim's freak *and* Bodenheim would READ A POEM—see, every time after a SESSION uh FUCKIN'!

PHAEDO: Oh for—

APOLLODOROS: And Aymes kinda got intrigued by that shit— and it got to where the poetry was BETTER than the PUSSY . . . and . . . well, as some of you may already know . . . in the winter of 1954 Bodenheim eventually married some girl and they picked up some crazy-ass dishwasher and the dishwasher fucked and STABBED the Bodenheim bitch to death, and SHOT Bodenheim dead in a room over on 12th Street and Third Avenue— **xli** Carl Sandburg sent flowers, beautiful homegoin' service, Praise God. And 'round 'bout that time, 1954, Aymes, who *could have been* about eighteen or twenty-eight, dependin' on who you wanna believe, he went off and found poetry after that! Now . . . I wasn't there . . . but I have *very* reputable sources who wrote poems and drank in bars *at that time*—and these friends pass the truth on to me and I carry the truth with me rolled up in my stockin's and stuffed down my bra for safe keepin'. —I know it ain't my turn but . . . well . . . you may continue.

(Apollodoros sashays upstage to make herself another drink.)

ION: Well . . . I've never heard this . . . *story* . . . of Aymes and Maxwell Bodenheim . . . but it is highly unlikely, and as you know, history abounds with gossip, rumor and folktales.

APOLLODOROS: That's the stuff history is made of—some *good shit*!

(Beat.)

THE MODERATOR: Meno . . .

MENO: Yes?

THE MODERATOR: I'm wondering . . . if—even if Aymes did help create his own celebrity, do you think, maybe, he quickly became uncomfortable with his celebrity, because he knew what celebrity meant to his art? I mean . . . do you think . . . maybe, when he sat down and wrote his book . . . did he know then that it was his celebrity that was about to distract his audience from his art, and any thesis or philosophy—thus, all he would be left with was his celebrity?

PHAEDO: He was a new figure, a new black writer, and—

MENO: Well . . . he was a *new* figure—and he *was* black . . . or *sort of black* . . . like Anatole Broyard . . . but not black like LeRoi Jones—

ION *(A joke that falls flat)*: Who after the '50s had become *very* black.

APOLLODOROS: Was the motherfucker Negro or was he black?

PHAEDO: Yes—let's be clear!

MENO: I don't know what he was! I don't care—he could've made a movie, he could've made a lot of money—he messed it all up.

THE MODERATOR: What do you mean he "messed it all up"? Messed what up?

MENO: He had a chance to make it! Like Kerouac!

THE MODERATOR: Like what?

MENO: MGM and Steve Allen paid a lot of money for the rights to Kerouac's first novel—

THE MODERATOR: What did any of that have to do with Aymes?

MENO: Kerouac also had a little abstract film out that year, *Pull My Daisy*, with the French actress—

ION: Delphine Seyrig.

PHAEDO: And correction, it was Robert Franck's film *based* on Kerouac's first novel—

THE MODERATOR: What, was it some kind of AN OPPORTU-NITY for you—to be like Steve Allen, to MAKE Aymes to be like KEROUAC!

MENO: Don't you put words in my mouth!

ION: Correction, it was *based* on an unfinished play of Kerouac's.

PHAEDO: Actually, the title of the film was borrowed from a collaborative poem Kerouac—

THE MODERATOR: I'm just trying to get clear! When a man writes a book, he's not thinking about being co-opted!

MENO: Oh for Christ's sake—

ION *(Finishing Phaedo's sentence)*: Neal Cassady and Allen Ginsberg published in *Neurotica* called *Pull My Daisy*.

THE MODERATOR: I don't care about *Pull My Daisy*!

PHAEDO: Actually the film was NOT based on anything except an aimless improvisation!

MENO: Listen, I didn't need him!

ION: Actually, it was not improvised, despite Kerouac's statements to the contrary.

MENO: He needed me!

THE MODERATOR: For WHAT? NEEDED YOU FOR WHAT?

ION *(To the audience)*: Kerouac's film would have a very important impact on Aymes, regarding the film he would eventually make of his own book, but I'll address that later.

PHAEDO *(Also to the audience)*: I disagree, and I will address that later!

THE MODERATOR: I DON'T CARE ABOUT *PULL MY DAISY*! Meno— *(Stands)* do you think you may have played a part in the death of the man?

MENO: I DIDN'T HAVE ANYTHING TO DO WITH THE DEATH OF THE MAN!

ΩΩ
≈
DITHYRAMB

(Intense light change. Apollodoros rises to her feet. Her voice is calm and steady, reverberating under the argument.)

APOLLODOROS:
> The United States of America, by and through David Goldblatt, United States Attorney for the District of New York, and Katherine Proffitt Mann and F. G. Hooper and Gayle Edsall, Assistant United States Attorneys . . . This memorandum respectfully submitted—

HUBRIS

PHAEDO: It is obvious this man is not interested in having a real dialogue about—

APOLLODOROS:
> Pleas and trials . . .

ION *(Defending Meno)*: What he's doing is bringing up the issue of art and the commodification of art, which is a relevant topic—

PHAEDO: IT IS IRRELEVANT!

ION: If you'd let him—

APOLLODOROS *(At the bottom of the stairs looking toward the balcony)*:
> The eighth superseding indictment charges twenty-five defendants, fourteen of whom have pled guilty. The trials for two of the eleven defendants who have not pled guilty have been severed for resolution at a later time. The remaining nine defendants are set for a joint trial to commence on August 5th of 1970.

THE MODERATOR *(Too personal)*: Do you—do you think . . . maybe it was a time for . . . celebrity? ONLY celebrity?

MENO: What? I don't . . .

PHAEDO *(Defending the Moderator)*: He is talking about gestures of living—about art that exists *outside* of the marketplace!

MENO: What's everybody so worked up about?

ION *(Again, referring to Meno)*: What he's doing is—

CRITO *(Accusing Meno; to Ion)*: No—what he's DOING—what he's bringing up is the same ol' BULLSHIT! The man always got some noble theory about how niggas supposed to make art and how that's supposed to make money—

ION: Oh, don't make this a race matter!

CRITO: I didn't make it a race matter!

PHAEDO: Art is a gesture of living. We make gestures of living. Gestures of living are habits of existence, and dying voluntarily implies the absence of profound reason!

ION: Lay off the booze, lady, you're not even coherent!

APOLLODOROS *(Climbing the stairs)*:
A grand jury returned the eight superseding indictments which charged the twenty-five defendants scheduled for trial, with offenses as described below:

PHAEDO: The absence of profound reason—if we can talk about that—

APOLLODOROS *(Intoning)*:
Disorderly conduct.

PHAEDO: About how the man lived—about why he *died*!

THE MODERATOR *(To Meno; transforming into someone else)*: You saw him . . . standing by that window . . . saw him catching the air . . . he just wanted the air . . . don't you understand that? Just wanted to catch the air . . .

APOLLODOROS:
>   Resisting arrest.

THE MODERATOR: He just wanted to get close enough to the fire . . .

APOLLODOROS:
>   Assault and battery.

THE MODERATOR: Didn't wanna get burned . . .

APOLLODOROS:
>   Vandalism.

THE MODERATOR: It was a dangerous place . . .

APOLLODOROS:
>   Involuntary manslaughter.

MENO: I don't know what was so dangerous?

THE MODERATOR: A dangerous thing . . .

MENO: You young people today have all these notions—everything's so *dangerous.*

CRITO: Everything *is.*

ION: I have some excerpts from the book I'm writing on Aymes—

PHAEDO: You've been writing it for twenty years!

ION: Moderator—if I may—

PHAEDO: I think we should move on to film. If you are to understand Archer, you must—

CRITO: It's all a hustle, baby, a dangerous hustle!

THE MODERATOR: The man wrote a book—wanted people to hear what he was saying!

MENO: Listen, don't you tell *me* about—

THE MODERATOR: Why was that so difficult?

MENO: PEOPLE just didn't GET IT!

APOLLODOROS *(Arriving at the balcony)*:
> The government and most defense counsel agree that stipulations are likely for at least some evidence and testimony . . .

(The panel—silent witnesses.)

THE MODERATOR: Well maybe Burroughs could get away with killing his wife—

APOLLODOROS:
> Categories of proof.

THE MODERATOR: And the Beats could say and do what they wanted to—could talk bad about the pipe-smoking forefathers in the spotlight—

APOLLODOROS:
> Matters not disputed.

THE MODERATOR: Because the forefathers were their fathers— NOT HIS!

APOLLODOROS *(Cradling the amphora)*:
> Potential stipulations include tape transcripts, handwriting exemplars, forensic comparisons and tests . . .

THE MODERATOR: And their controversies would only fuel their celebrity—prolong it—while Aymes would always be just another colored entertainer, tap-dancing in the wings!

APOLLODOROS:
> Qualifications of experts.

MENO: Aymes wasn't in the wings—he was on the main stage! The MAIN STAGE! I should know—I PUT HIM THERE. And *everybody* was tap-dancing in the '50s!

THE MODERATOR: —ALL ONE BIG FINALE!

APOLLODOROS *(Descending, carrying the amphora)*:
In the case of Archer Aymes . . . Having organized protest without a permit . . .

MENO: We ALL had a SALES GIMMICK! Aymes had his OWN gimmick—HIMSELF! He worked AGAINST his own gimmick! I mean, for God's sake, what he was so damned angry—RIGHT FROM THE START—I DON'T KNOW!

APOLLODOROS:
Having caused death . . .

THE MODERATOR: Maybe he was practicing death—like Lara somebody or other!

MENO: Here he is—praised for his first literary effort at the age twenty-nine!

APOLLODOROS:
Having been born American . . .

THE MODERATOR: Three—he was twenty-three!

MENO: He was TALKED ABOUT! The new important Negro in modern letters—and what did he do with it? What did it all mean?

THE MODERATOR: What *did it* mean—this new Negro importance in modern letters?

APOLLODOROS:
Having been born black . . .

MENO: I don't know what you're—

THE MODERATOR: New as opposed to old—did you trust this newness?

APOLLODOROS:
    Having made art for art's sake . . .

MENO: YOU don't know what you're talking—

THE MODERATOR: Did the people who wanted to meet him? Did they trust the oldness?

MENO: That's very funny—no . . . I—

THE MODERATOR: So when you say—*new*—is it a put-down? Some kind of *coded language* sent out to the masses?

APOLLODOROS:
    In a time of war.

MENO: I'm not sure where you're going with this. It's not important whether or not—

APOLLODOROS:
    Having unlawfully entered the Museum of Antiquities . . .
    In search of himself . . .

THE MODERATOR: Important—relative only to newness. Otherwise unimportant—Negro—not white—colored—marginal—trivial. Was he trivial? Was he new? Was he colored? Was he trivial *because* he was *new* and *colored*?

MENO: LISTEN—WHAT THE HELL ARE YOU UP TO—

APOLLODOROS (*Approaching Meno from behind*):
    In search of his mother.

MENO (*To the audience*): You know, my mother was an actress in the Yiddish theatres on the Lower East Side—Ibsen, Tolstoy, Brecht, in Yiddish . . .

THE MODERATOR: No—I don't care—

MENO: My father was a vaudevillian, doin' little bits here and

there all over the death trail—

THE MODERATOR: That's NOT what we're—

MENO: Pulled me and mother into his act from the time I could
aim my own ding-a-ling and piss into a pot—

THE MODERATOR: THIS IS NOT ABOUT YOU—

APOLLODOROS:
In need . . .

MENO: I worked everywhere from Harlem nightclubs to Café
Society, and what was so dangerous?

THE MODERATOR: YOU DIDN'T HAVE TO COMPETE
WITH—

MENO: WE ALL HAD TO COMPETE—WITH SOME-
THING—*THE BLOB* OR ELVIS PRESLEY!

APOLLODOROS *(Stands directly behind Meno)*:
In need of resolve!

THE MODERATOR: NO, I NEED—I'M ASKING YOU—
ABOUT AYMES—

MENO: And we had a great time!

THE MODERATOR: WHAT ABOUT—NO—

MENO: We had a GREAT time!

THE MODERATOR: NO—THAT'S NOT WHAT I'M SAYING!
NO—WHAT I'M SAYING IS—NO—

MENO: A GREAT time!

(Apollodoros lifts the amphora above Meno's head.)

THE MODERATOR: NO!

(She motions as if to hurl it down onto his skull.)

THE MODERATOR *(Seeing what she is about to do)*: NOOOOOOO!!!

Ω

(Silence. All turn to Apollodoros. She smiles. Meno sits, not sure of what almost happened. Nervous tension. Apollodoros balances the amphora on her head. Another presentation for the audience:)

APOLLODOROS: Exhibit E: Large-belly amphora. Cadmus is *old* xlv
. . . he offers the young Pentheus a wreath of ivy for xlvi
his head, and invites him to worship his God. Pentheus *refuses* his gift of ivy. Pentheus refuses his God. I thought . . . *you* . . . might be interested in taking a closer look at this one . . . *dear* Moderator.

(She seats the amphora at table center. She returns to her place at the table, crosses her legs. Beat.)

THE MODERATOR: Uh . . . thank you . . . Apollodoros. *(His attention on Apollodoros, he removes the vase, places it on the floor, unsure of himself and the moment)* Meno . . . please accept my apologies. I . . . this is not my intention . . . to argue . . . but . . . I guess I . . . I don't understand. I mean . . . it sounds to me . . . like . . . well, you say you met Aymes when he was a nobody. Ten years later you see him at a party when he's at the beginning of his celebrity, he dismisses you, every time you see him after that he snaps at you, makes it very clear to you that he's not interested in the world you say he was a part of. Yet you insist on him being on your show because Hollywood was going to make a movie of his book . . . because he was the new Kerouac? And he accepts? That . . . that . . . just— doesn't make any sense to me.

(Beat.)

MENO: Tell me somethin' kid . . . what—is Aymes some kind
of hero to you or somethin'?

THE MODERATOR *(His attention still focused on Apollodoros)*:
No—well yes . . . I . . . I mean . . . what I mean to say is
I—

MENO: Are all your heroes dead?

THE MODERATOR: What?

MENO: Your heroes—are all of your heroes dead?

THE MODERATOR: I—

MENO: Why you're so worked up about a man who made a
mess of everything—all before your time—you're too
young to be looking that far back.

THE MODERATOR: Give me something to look forward to.

(Beat.)

MENO: . . . I'm a dying man.

MODULE 2

Museum of the Perpetual,
Death of the Hero, Immortality of the Soul:
A Triadic Progression

A movie is literally a series of images, and what one sees in a movie can really be taken . . . as the key to what the movie is actually involved in saying . . . in Hollywood, for example, immortality and evil (which are synonyms in that lexicon) are always vividly punished, though it is the way of the transgressor—which keeps us on the edge of our seats—and the transgressor himself who engages all our sympathy.　　—JAMES BALDWIN

Love is the oldest of gods . . . there can be no greater benefit for a boy than to have a worthy lover . . . nor for a lover than to have a worthy object for his affection . . .　　　　　　　　　　　—PHAEDO

Music: violin and piano; Arvo Pärt's Alina; Spiegel im Spiegal.

ΩΩ

(Phaedo stands facing out, holding a screenplay. Grainy black-and-white images project against the surface of her body, gradually enlarging onto the wall behind her—consuming the space. She is extremely focused, meditative—revisiting her life in the body of a long-lost lover. The Moderator, seated slightly upstage of her, also faces out, searching the text of Mother and Son *as he looks to the film. Apollodoros walks through, quietly invading a dream.)*

PHAEDO: Visual language: facial expressions, tone of voice, gestures. Films were once called photoplays, inheriting the traditions of novels—but they are visual novels. It makes perfect sense that he would translate a novel into a film. You must follow the pages of the book carefully as the images unfold before you. We used super-8, projecting at eighteen frames per second—with an automatic light meter and battery-driven motor. We filmed in black-and-white to get the tones of charcoal drawings. We used natural light to capture the essence of great paintings by the Impressionists. A wide-angle lens was sometimes used. As the lens widens the perspective, it creates a depth of distortion.

APOLLODOROS: Embrace the distortion of reality.

PHAEDO: He was an artist. Other writers have made films— like the great French Surrealist Antonin Artaud—but Aymes was not *just* a writer—

APOLLODOROS: He was an *artist.*

PHAEDO: He painted with words and images. Aymes actually painted onto some of the film. He took old film, washed off the emulsion using Clorox—and wearing rubber gloves, we wiped off the film with a soft cloth to expose the clear acetate. We fastened the filmstrip to a dining room table with masking tape. On 8-millimeter we painted stripes and vertical strokes, using indelible felt-tipped markers and acetate inks with brushes. For some shots, we scratched the film—using a stylus. Tiny lines spliced in several frames. We did not use sound. The film was twenty-two minutes and thirty-eight seconds long. As you read the book, and look back to the images—something happens to you between the space of words and image.

xlvii

(Reciting the text from the screenplay, without referring to it:)

EXTERIOR. OCEAN. NIGHT.

—Where are you?

THE MODERATOR: I'm on page thirty-four, when the mother arrives on these shores for the first time.

APOLLODOROS: And I, Apollodoros—eighteen years of age, the year of Santana's *Abraxas* . . . I had just hung Santana's *Black Magic Woman* on my wall—black woman with a white dove feeding from her pussy . . . congas clutched between her thighs, reclining on Egyptian velvet. And I, Apollodoros, had just told the gods I would be that woman with a psychedelic angel hovering above me . . .

PHAEDO *(Describing what she sees)*:
    AERIAL VIEW OF A SHIP
    moving across an enormous body of water.
    ANOTHER SHOT of an island in the distance.
    CLOSE-UP on a young woman's hands.
    They are young hands but worn.
    She is about sixteen years of age—
    She is a woman, not a girl.
    EXTREME CLOSE-UP of her face.
    These SHOTS of her face, hands, the ship, the island—
    repeat in succession.
    INTERIOR. GREAT HALL.
    A large and derelict hall,
    suggesting Ellis Island's Immigration Hall.
    It is abandoned.
    Young woman enters abandoned hall.

THE MODERATOR: There is no Ellis Island or place of immigration in the book at all. I'm curious as to why—

PHAEDO: We are all immigrants from one experience into the next. It is about transference. A young woman comes to a new land on a great ship from somewhere. Comes across water, which makes her something like a *Christ* figure—walking on water—*walking* across it.

APOLLODOROS: And I, Apollodoros, seated in the room of my mother and father's Tudor house beneath a poster of Vietnamese children killed in the My Lai massacre— March 16th 1968—my poster, which I had cut out from an article in *Life* magazine. Question: And babies? Answer: And babies.

PHAEDO: In process—in this journey across water—once she's arrived on the shores of promise, she becomes part of a work force . . . and not long thereafter she is pregnant. This hall represents the point of transition, where agreement is made. One agrees to enter into a *new world*, has journeyed far to get to it—and here it is. Is it all of what was hoped for? Is it enough?

APOLLODOROS: . . . And I, Apollodoros, wept many a night beneath massacred Vietnamese children galvanizing anti-war sentiment . . . on my bedroom wall.

PHAEDO:
    EXTERIOR. MARKETPLACE. DAY.
    CLOSE-UP of fruits,
    vegetables,
    garments,
    pushcarts . . .
    Tenement buildings.
    The woman stands, holding a piece of fruit in her hand.
    The marketplace bustles around her.
    CLOSE-UP on bruised fruit.
    INTERIOR. ROOM. DAY.
    A cot.
    A dresser.
    A chair.
    A cross.
    A flag.
    CLOSE-UP of Jesus on the cross.
    CUT TO woman lying on bed.
    She is contorting and writhing in pain.
    DISSOLVE TO cross, falling from wall.
    Sheets covered in blood.
    SHOT of nude woman with a baby
    resting on her stomach.
    CLOSE-UP of the infant.

He is dark-skinned, with dark curly hair.
Very dark.
VARIOUS SHOTS of
the infant's hands, feet, genitalia.
CLOSE-UP on his face,
looking at her . . . smiling.
CLOSE-UP on her face,
looking at him . . . smiling.

THE MODERATOR: In the book, the conception of the son is not mentioned—and in the film, the conception is not shown—or even suggested—

PHAEDO: Rendering it immaculate. An *immaculate* conception.

THE MODERATOR: Yes, but what is the purpose of this in the—

PHAEDO: Perhaps she has married . . . or fallen in love . . . one cannot know . . . but the virgin immigrant is soon pregnant. A deified immigrant of virtue walks across water in one frame; a menial laborer (a seller of fruit) in the next; a pregnant woman (a mother) in the next . . .

APOLLODOROS: Sneaking out at night to Greenwich Village to the theatres and bars of the Lower East Side—and to Harlem—to see the plays of Adrienne Kennedy and Amiri Baraka and Ed Bullins again . . . to say thank you or curse them out for that last line in the second act. To hear Olu Dara or Miles with the Dead at the Fillmore East . . . to catch Ornette Coleman—once—just sitting at the bar or walking home after the gig. To let them know my pussy had doves perched at its clit and I was an eighteen-year-old goddess who was not afraid of a little weed or some blow if you got it, and all I have to give the world one day will be a dance or a song or a poem or a play . . . or my pussy . . . to Sly Stone if he will have me.

PHAEDO:

INTERIOR. ROOM. NIGHT.

—Where are you now?

THE MODERATOR: Page ten. The mother teaches the boy to walk.

PHAEDO:

The boy—he is about two years of age, nude.

He is holding onto the woman as he takes his first steps.

CLOSE-UP of his small feet as he walks

over a cross with Jesus.

Boy falls.

CLOSE-UP of boy's face as he cries.

CLOSE-UP of the mother's face as she cries.

SHOT of dark-skinned boy sitting on the floor, crying.

Mother stands in front of him, crying . . .

There is some distance between them here.

—Where are you?

THE MODERATOR: Page two.

And already she missed him and sobbed at the great distance between them as he lay on her breast—new and growing old and covered in blood . . .

PHAEDO:

EXTERIOR. MARKETPLACE. DAY.

THE MODERATOR:

She was there and he was there, in the great marketplace. She had come to sell and he had come to help her sell. He had come to see. He had come to play.

PHAEDO:

He had come to vanish into the sea . . .

PHAEDO AND THE MODERATOR:

Of the marketplace and its bustling—

THE MODERATOR: What is the significance of this—the mother working, and the son vanishing into the crowd?

PHAEDO: He is a man now. Sons, when they grow older, as they enter into manhood, they are like lovers. They are men.

APOLLODOROS: Women fall in love with these men—

PHAEDO: Women . . . grow old in the process of loving men, and still they are reduced to girlhood . . . even the women who have mothered and nurtured men from infancy to their elder years. The women grow old and coquettish. The men grow disinterested. And like lovers—these young men lose interest in the women who have mothered and nurtured them. They are distracted. They vanish . . .

> EXTERIOR. VACANT LOT. DAY.
> A young man roams the hillsides.
> He is white, with dark curly hair.
> Discovers America.
> He discovers. His mother works.

THE MODERATOR: The boy is born *colored*—as a teenager he is white?

PHAEDO: He is born in a tight place. Born inside a room of walls.

THE MODERATOR: But the mother, she doesn't change color. She's always white. Why?

PHAEDO: Archer said . . . her perpetual whiteness was a character flaw.

APOLLODOROS: Having only heard of this man, this poet, who had written this book, many years before, this man who had written these words I cared so much for . . . these words I felt like I had written upon first reading them . . . And when I watched him on television, carried in the arms of policemen, quoting Albert Camus—and fell in love—beautiful. Then the man himself, saw him there, sitting in that bar, clothes ripped, dried blood, swollen eyes fainting, slumped over, bare feet—beautiful . . .

PHAEDO:

    Teenage boy stands at one end of the vacant lot.
    A young girl stands at the other end, eating a piece of fruit.
    Boy approaches young girl.
    CLOSE-UP on boy's face . . .

APOLLODOROS: Full of discovery.

PHAEDO:

    CLOSE-UP on girl's face—

APOLLODOROS: Ripe with invitation. And she said to him . . . excuse me . . . I do not know you . . . but I have something to say to you—a poet who has written words I felt like I had written—a maker of dreams . . . I am an eighteen-year-old goddess with doves perched at my clit and wasn't it you who said?—she said—you who said Camus said:

    Thus each of us had to be content to live only for the day, alone under the vast indifference of the sky. This sense of being abandoned? . . .

PHAEDO:

    INTERIOR. ROOM. DAY.
    The mother, she is alone now.
    She is much older now.
    She is a girl, not a woman.
    CUT TO Jesus on the cross.
    CUT TO woman kneeling in prayer.
    CUT TO woman lying on bed.
    CUT TO woman contorting, and writhing in pain.
    CUT TO cross, falling from wall.

CUT TO Jesus lying on sheets.
CUT TO sheets covered in blood.
CUT TO woman lying on sheets with Jesus.
CUT TO baby resting on her stomach.
CUT TO various shots of his face, his hands.
CLOSE-UP of woman's face . . .
Looking at him . . .

THE MODERATOR: We've gone backwards, to the beginning.

PHAEDO: Yes. A flashback—to first love . . . when relationships are new and covered in blood.

APOLLODOROS: And he smiled and placed his finger at her mouth—and finished it,

> in this extremity of solitude none could count for any help from his neighbor . . . Each had to bear the weight of his troubles alone.

And she placed a finger at his mouth—and finished it,

> if by some chance one of us tried to unburden himself or say something about his feelings, the reply he got, whatever it might be, usually wounded him. Whether friendly or hostile, the reply always missed fire . . . and the attempt to communicate had to be given up, however heavy our hearts . . .

PHAEDO:

> . . . For all our emptiness . . .

APOLLODOROS:

> . . . the attempt to communicate had to be given up . . . had to.

THE MODERATOR: So . . . what is being said?

PHAEDO: The subject of her desire is the space she inhabits. The object of her desire is her emptiness. The emptiness of space.

APOLLODOROS: And I knew then there would be no art to come for some and perhaps there would be for others, but it would have to be a war, if it were to occur—art—a war . . . And there would be slaughtered babies—if it were to come—and I knew he must die if he were to leave anything worth remembering . . . And I must carry his . . . his offering . . . I . . . I would give birth to his child—and give it away, to survive or be massacred.

PHAEDO: One is not a woman . . . until one knows desire—the danger of desire. She must acknowledge this in her walking.

APOLLODOROS: And we walked . . . continued walking . . . to a small room in a Tudor house . . . lay beneath massacred Vietnamese children . . . an eighteen-year-old goddess reclining on Egyptian velvet, giving herself to a poet. No words. Only sound.

PHAEDO *(Softly, as if to Archer)*: Where are you now?

THE MODERATOR *(Closes the book)*: I've lost my place. Where is the son?

PHAEDO: He is gone.

APOLLODOROS: The son is gone.

PHAEDO: Now there is only one woman . . . the girl . . .

APOLLODOROS: The mother . . .

PHAEDO: Herself . . . and this endless walking she does . . .

APOLLODOROS: . . . we do . . .

PHAEDO: . . . seems perpetual, we never stop.

APOLLODOROS: We continue walking . . . endless walking . . .

PHAEDO: trying to come closer to . . .

APOLLODOROS: but moving farther away from . . .

PHAEDO: each other . . . moving closer to danger.

THE MODERATOR: And desire?

PHAEDO: They are the same thing.

THE MODERATOR: So, are the girl and the mother the same thing?
PHAEDO: Danger and desire.
PHAEDO AND APOLLODOROS: They are the same thing.

Ω

(The screen goes dark, they return to the conference table.)

THE MODERATOR: If you don't mind, I'd like to ask you about the film—you said Archer Aymes was a real artist who knew that "real life retreated into dreams." What exactly do you mean—

PHAEDO *(Slow recovery, answering the question, not necessarily his)*: Maya Deren employed the logic of dreams. She [xlviii] was a maker of dreams—died suddenly—sucked up into a dream . . . One writer said her films possessed "the taste of a mid-winter sky with the shining blade of a ceremonial knife sticking out of the moon's blood." I sat there . . . at the Cherry Lane, watching the films of Stan Brakhage, Jonas Mekas, Len Lye, Godard . . . sat there in the dark, not a woman, a girl . . . a silly little girl of jingling bracelets with a new shade of red on my mouth and a handbag from Paris . . . sat there, being beautiful in the dark . . . wondering, what does it matter when you are beautiful in the dark if no one can see you? Perhaps in the dark, the only thing that matters is what *you* see . . . and I saw . . . Maya Deren's *Meshes of the Afternoon* . . . I saw . . . multiple selves, each self [xlix] observing the life of the other . . . each self performing the same act the prior self had performed—we are not one person.
APOLLODOROS: We are many.
PHAEDO *(An epiphany, acknowledging Apollodoros)*: In a film . . . like in a mirror . . . we see the others. I saw the others, myself . . . and was possessed . . . Archer saw me in a

film I had done in Paris, *Outremer*, and was possessed . . . I read his book and was possessed . . . we met each other, there, in the throes of self-possession . . .

(Meno groans.)

THE MODERATOR: Phaedo, I was looking at your film, following along in the book as you told me, and I don't understand—

PHAEDO: You *must* . . . understand . . . how entwined our process was . . . you see, we edited *Mother and Son* at Dionysus—

MENO: Dionysus?

PHAEDO: He named it Dionysus after the Greek god Dionysus—

APOLLODOROS: A god whose worship causes the loss of individual identity.

PHAEDO: And identity is central to the themes Aymes explored in his work . . . the loss of it and the recovery of it.

THE MODERATOR: Where was the Dionysus Film Center?

PHAEDO: We never had a building or an office of our own. We operated, primarily, from my apartment on West 4th Street . . . Archer loved my apartment because it had once been occupied by the great black actor, Canada Lee—

MENO: Hitchcock's *Lifeboat*!

PHAEDO: Lee died before he accomplished what he truly wanted to with his art . . . Archer said Lee always felt like he was on the "verge of something."

THE MODERATOR: So Dionysus was based in your apartment?

PHAEDO: No . . . well . . . Archer and I were walking through Manhattan. I was telling Archer about my childhood . . . the servants in livery, my mother's dreadful weekly teas . . . and we were standing outside of an old abandoned building . . . a mansion of some sort . . . paused outside of its gate . . . he asked me if the house I had grown up in was as big as this building . . . I said, no, of course not.

THE MODERATOR: This building—

PHAEDO: It was gargantuan . . . one of those old dinosaurs from the Victorian era . . . and he . . . oddly enough, he said he had grown up in similar settings.

ION: That's not true.

PHAEDO: "The important truth is the poetic one." —Maya Deren!

THE MODERATOR: Did Aymes mean he grew up in a mansion in Mississippi or Brooklyn?

CRITO: What do *you* think?

PHAEDO: I didn't take him seriously, rather, I didn't take what he said *literally.*

APOLLODOROS: Why not?

THE MODERATOR: What do you mean?

PHAEDO: One day, he said, we will occupy this building, learn its secrets. Archer fantasized that the old building would be our center, our Dionysus.

APOLLODOROS: The building . . . do you remember where it was?

PHAEDO: No—but it's not important. If you are to understand *Mother and Son* you must understand what we intended to achieve at Dionysus. When I left New York for Paris it was unheard of that a woman should want to become a filmmaker. There was no room for my artistic expression . . . even in France. I was an artist, in search of an artistic theory—but the art of France had been ruined by war . . . Archer said war was probably the most important social contribution to the environment of art, because art is the only thing war can bring life to. Funny . . . it never leaves you does it?

THE MODERATOR: What?

PHAEDO: That moment . . . when you first fell in love with a voice . . . a face . . . the twilight of alchemy . . . it's with you forever.

MENO: "Reg-yu-lar-lee . . ."

PHAEDO: In France, I'd met François Truffaut . . . he was interested in casting me in *Les Quatre Cent Coup*. It was a favorite of not only mine, but Archer's. I had fallen in love with the work of François Truffaut, and his refusal to use film for humanistic ends . . . his need to . . . to create a disparity between what is said and what we see.

ION *(Interrupting)*: Truffaut chronicled the thirteenth year in a child's life, and—

PHAEDO *(Refusing to be interrupted)*: Archer's film chronicled the lifelong relationship between a mother and son. The images are pieces of evidence—

APOLLODOROS *(Pointedly, to the Moderator)*: Indicators of time . . . marking the path toward death.

lii ION: Gillain!

MENO: Abstract mishmash!

PHAEDO *(Reaching out to the Moderator)*: A mother . . . gives her child the illusion of an external reality . . . which corresponds with the infant's desire to create, and the first creative impulse of the child is the transitional *object*—a toy— which can only be found in the external world. And the external world teaches the child that there is a transitional

liii space he can inhabit, a playground . . . literary environs . . .

MENO: A psychiatric ward. . . .

APOLLODOROS: But if the child is *deprived* of maternal care, he or she *loses* the ability to relate . . .

PHAEDO: Yes . . . to the external world.

THE MODERATOR: And . . . a sense of danger . . . replaces a sense of trust?

PHAEDO, APOLLODOROS AND ION: Yes.

ION: And that is *Mother and Son*—the book and the film, are about Aymes's inability to relate to the external world. It's autobiographical, like Truffaut!

PHAEDO: No—you are sooo out of your league with me— Truffaut's films are NOT autobiographical! Autobiographies are *obituary* in their nature!

ION: Sartre!

PHAEDO: Gillain locates Truffaut's films as coming from the "script of delinquency," which relies on effects, not **liv** events! Subversive memory! In his film, Aymes—like Truffaut—*subverts* chronological order!

ION: He's not the only one.

THE MODERATOR: Phaedo, you were about to explain the influence of the French New Wave and the experimental film movement on Archer.

PHAEDO: I was?

THE MODERATOR: Yes.

ION *(Under)*: Louis Malle . . . Molinaro . . .

PHAEDO: Well . . . they were not really an influence on Archer. *I* was his influence.

ION: Philippe de Broca . . . Jacques Rivette . . . Godard . . . Goran.

PHAEDO: The French New Wave was a great influence on *me*, but it was still a patriarchal system . . . oppressive . . . not until I became exposed to the women filmmakers: Germaine Dulac, Marguerite Duras—

THE MODERATOR: Maya Deren . . .

PHAEDO: Yes—you see, I realized it was *women* who were liberating film from illusionist Hollywood representations of women. Women who—

MENO: Dykes and bulldaggers.

PHAEDO: Women who were developing a *semiotic* cinema and giving voice to the voiceless . . . and this is the most important thing Archer and I had in common.

THE MODERATOR: Race and gender?

PHAEDO: And the artistic process of both. We were no different, Archer and I. His black male body. My white female body—it was the same body . . .

MENO: *Huh?*

ION: The first logical thing she's said all evening! Black bodies, white bodies . . . Aymes . . . *(To the audience)* If you look at Cassavetes' *Shadows*—it's about siblings who seem virtually raceless, passing for white, BUT—

PHAEDO *(Cutting him off)*: THAT is not what *Shadows* is about—Cassavetes' characters are not allowed the pre-pubescent anarchical narcissism of blaming their psychosis on existing systems of knowledge—like Kerouac! The enemy is not without—it is within! That's what *Shadows* is about and this is equal to Archer's beliefs!

ION: How is that equal to Aymes's beliefs?

PHAEDO: He championed the eradication of our *instinctual* and *internalized* desire to elevate some forms of art above others—

ION: Aymes championed the abolishment of a Western or European influence on art!

PHAEDO: He was NOT against European or Western art!

ION: So then you agree with me that he was influenced by it?

PHAEDO: I do NOT agree with YOU!

ION *(Searching through his texts)*: Aymes was trying to be a multiculturalist and what's unfortunate about that was said best by Ray Carney—

CRITO: You got some shit with you, don't you?

ION: Ray Carney wrote:
   What most multiculturalists—

PHAEDO: DO NOT QUOTE—

ION:
   What most multiculturalists overlook in their attacks on the European and Western canon is that supreme works of genius in the Western tradition are often more hospitable to minority sentiments—

PHAEDO: DO NOT QUOTE RAY CARNEY TO ME!

(A boxing match.)

ION:

—MORE HOSPITABLE TO MINORITY SENTIMENTS than works EXPLICITLY minority-oriented.

PHAEDO: Most of what Ray Carney knows he learned from *me*. THE MOST IMPORTANT, being that critics such as yourself have no real language for criticism because you pay attention only to *systematic* ways of interpreting art when in fact the only way to interpret art is by deciphering the *emotional pulse* of it, *the undercurrent of spirit that embodies art.* You have NO language and you have NO spirit!

ION *(Slamming his text down, standing)*: What I have is two Ph.D.s, thirty years of experience, common sense, and my sanity! HOW ABOUT YOU, LADY?

PHAEDO: I HAVE TENURE!!!

(Group explosion. Applause.)

Ta gueule! S'applaudir! Complexe d'inferiorite!

ION: In English!

MENO: Louder! Faster! *Funnier!*

ION: It's no wonder Aymes left you to get SHOT AT in the segregated South!

(Another group explosion.)

You know this is all very interesting—fascinating actually. Is anyone keeping minutes, because I think this is really fascinating—I had no idea how firmly my theories would be supported by your statements, but I always had certain suspicions about the authenticity of

lvii   that film. Recontextualization. Aymes was replicating and sampling, borrowing and reproducing—and *being* sampled and reproduced by Phaedo—you know . . .

(To the audience) This brings me to the implausibility of postmodernism. Postmodernism, according to Fredric Jameson—I'm writing a book on Jameson—is supposed to be an "erosion of separations and distinctions between high culture and so-called mass or popu-

lviii   lar culture." That's all. But it wasn't enough for Aymes. Aymes wanted to blur the lines between high art and what was considered new and controversial—a stream-of-consciousness verse, an avant-garde film, produced from dreams and identity conflict—all the while he was still looking for some artistic act of political activism. It's all quite fascinating.

PHAEDO: What the HELL are you talking about? The film *was* an act of politicism!

ION: *Your* politicism—not his—the politics of you and the others at Dionysus who completed that film and entered it into the festival. Aymes didn't come back to New York until after the film had opened at the Greenwich Theatre and received the Bunuel Prize. Several people

lix   tried to interview him, but Aymes was incoherent—he barely knew anything about the film—that's why he abandoned it!

PHAEDO: You know NOTHING about it! He didn't *abandon* the film! He simply retreated into a small cave to try and see the world . . .

ION: He went to Marks, Mississippi! He went to Marks, Mississippi, to join the Mule Train! He went to Marks, Mississippi—he was searching for a way to art and political activism. You know, this is really fascinating—I'd seen the film but I was not convinced then that the film was really the work of Aymes—it seemed *very* different from the book—

PHAEDO: It was NOT DIFFERENT from the book—it was the *completion* of the book! I won't be accused of lying!

THE MODERATOR: No one is accusing you—

ION: Perhaps someone is. He barely had anything to do with the production of it. He told me so when I interviewed him in Marks, Mississippi, on the Mule Train.

PHAEDO: You were not in Marks, Mississippi, when Aymes was there—it is not possible—

THE MODERATOR: Crito, did Archer say anything to you, about the film—on the Mule Train?

CRITO *(To Ion)*: Funny this is just comin' up. That obituary you read, the one *you* wrote—you didn't say *nothin'* about the Mule Train in that obituary!

ION: I didn't think it relevant to his obituary in 1970! It wasn't an expedition he completed!

PHAEDO: You were the author of that obituary and it is an obituary of lies!

ION: I am the author of the obituary, not the lies! I have thirty years as a literary critic! I've published FOUR biographies—obviously I know how to fact-check! I met Aymes in 1968 when he first went to Marks. I was covering the event for the *Village Voice*—

CRITO: No—wait a minute—first of all—

ION: Archer was there, in Marks—a protest march—an absurd one at that—

CRITO: I don't see what was so absurd about it. I'm from Marks!

ION: Oooh, I know you are, sir!

CRITO: If you're gonna talk about the Mule Train and Marks, you have to explain what that . . . what that was all about—

THE MODERATOR: If you don't mind, Crito, I'd like to ask you some questions about the Mule—

ION: I think I was about to . . . I was *about* to talk about *Aymes's* involvement—

CRITO: I'm not talking about Aymes—I know about Aymes—

ION: This panel is about Aymes—

CRITO: You can't stand there and start your thing off until you explain what the people—what they were doing down there in Marks in the first place—

ION *(Threateningly)*: Oh—I intend to, Crito! I INTEND to explain EXACTLY what he was doing down there in Marks!

MENO *(Over them until everyone is quiet)*: YACK, YACK, YACK, YACK . . . You know . . . we sit here and fight over a man . . . a man who didn't give a shit about himself. Sit here on a crime scene, and talk about a man who didn't give a shit if he lived or died—didn't give a shit about anybody. Didn't know how to be grateful for the chance people were trying to give him. I mean I spent money, good money on optioning that goddamned book—

THE MODERATOR: You optioned the what?

CRITO: The book! The book, baby, the book!

PHAEDO: I wondered how long it would take . . .

MENO: You couldn't have made that stupid little movie of yours if my option on the book hadn't run out . . . Aymes knew that . . . ten years . . . made that little piece of shit to spite me . . . you think I don't know that? Steve Allen produced Jack's movie . . . Susskind produced *Requiem for a Heavyweight*! Aymes had a chance! I was on HIS side—I had been talking to very influential people in Hollywood who were interested . . . told him that night at the Y, at the train station . . . here's your chance kid, I've optioned the rights . . . I'm talking to people . . . he's arguing with me—says he doesn't want a movie— I tell him it's too late, I put out good money!

THE MODERATOR: So . . . he *had* to come on the show . . .

MENO: Says he'll come if he can write the screenplay . . . we shook on it . . . and it wasn't easy convincing the big boys, lemme tell you . . . all he has to do is come on the show . . .

talk about the book . . . read from it . . . but he comes on with these two novels that had just been published . . . uh—

ION: *Black as Night* by Daniel Nern and *A Place without Twilight* by Peter Feibleman.

MENO: Sittin' there, waving the books around—

ION: You see, they're both written by white men *about* black people—

MENO: Raging on and on about it, saying when will it stop?

ION: The critics said Nern was a "pretty good Negro writer," because he "hadn't written another Negro problem novel!" Note—Nern was white.

MENO: I don't know what to say, the audience is lookin' at him like he's crazy. I try to laugh it off, then he rages on about Mailer, saying Mailer is a drunk and the Beats are all junkies, and Hollywood is bullshit—here we are, LIVE! Says he's not gonna go to Hollywood and lie to people—he's a Negro, he can't afford to tell little white lies! The man was supposed to get on the plane the next day—Hollywood—these people are watching! America is watching, and he's turning everybody off, burning all his bridges . . . well we go to commercial break . . . he storms off to the green room, he's supposed to come back and read from his book, nobody knows what's goin' on with him . . .

PHAEDO: Sabotage—that's what was going on with him! Archer showed me the beginnings of the first draft of the screenplay he'd written in Hollywood . . . he wanted my opinion of it . . . I was judgmental, very harsh.

THE MODERATOR: Why?

MENO: Aymes's first drafts made no sense at all!

PHAEDO: There were a million fingerprints all over it—few of them his. He'd kept it locked away in a small metal box beneath his desk. It was typewritten and covered with little notes written in the margins. Lines drawn across the pages—

MENO: Tried to make sense out of it!

PHAEDO: It was full of other people's ideas—not his.

MENO: He didn't have any ideas!

PHAEDO: It appealed to the logical, the succinct—very predictable in its structure—full of lines and words that could not have come from a man who had written the book that I read—

MENO: They even hired Dalton Trumbo to try and make some sense out of it—

CRITO *(Very dry)*: Communist—blacklisted by McCarthy.

MENO: He wrote *Spartacus*!

PHAEDO: I told him that I thought it was . . . unfortunate, that his identity had been tortured this way.

MENO: Oh for God's sake.

PHAEDO: That his art—his mind—had not been trusted . . .

MENO: Blah blah blah.

PHAEDO: That his body had been purchased and then violated . . . You could see it in his face. The damage. He was a man whose words had been taken away from him—and he was trying to get them back. He was intrigued by this put-down, and our constant war of words. He said I sparred well . . . with words.

ION: Of which you must be very proud.

THE MODERATOR: So the two of you rewrote his screenplay?

PHAEDO: We did NOT write or rewrite a screenplay! We sketched our storyboard on the ceiling of my apartment, like the constellations . . . painted it in bright colors, and we'd lay in bed, looking up at the ceiling . . . waking up to our film . . . sleeping beneath it . . . we never wrote a screenplay. When we finally achieved a complete storyboard, I told him he had made something magnificent . . . told him he reminded me of Luis Bunuel. Simply in his aesthetic. His natural ability to take the natural and make it unnatural but familiar.

ION: Again—and *who* directed?

PHAEDO: Archer directed!

ION: Asked you to be in it?

PHAEDO: And at first I said no!

THE MODERATOR AND CRITO: Why?

PHAEDO: He said I was his muse. I became agitated, told him I did not want to be that—would not be like one of the tragic beauties fueling the genius of god-like men. He never brought it up again . . . and then . . . well . . . I found my way into it.

ION: *Found* your way into it?

PHAEDO: I knew the pulse of it—how the role should be performed.

ION: But before the film was completed, Archer *abandoned* the project, yes?

PHAEDO: No! He did not abandon it!

THE MODERATOR: But he didn't complete it either—did he?

PHAEDO: Complete . . . no, he did not *complete* it . . . *(Beat)* He . . . he left while we were in the middle of production—

THE MODERATOR: To go to Mississippi, to go to Marks?

ION: That's where, not why! I'll tell you why he left—

PHAEDO: YOU KNOW NOTHING ABOUT IT!

THE MODERATOR: Phaedo, if it was really *his* film . . . why did he leave . . . in the middle of production?

PHAEDO: I don't know.

THE MODERATOR *(Accusatory)*: You don't know? Did the man have anything to do with the film at all?

PHAEDO: You . . . you don't *believe* . . . you mustn't believe—

THE MODERATOR: I don't know what to believe!

CRITO *(Angrily at the Moderator)*: She's talking to you! Tryin' to tell you somethin'!

THE MODERATOR: I heard what she had to say—

CRITO: You DIDN'T hear!

THE MODERATOR: She made a movie, signed his name to it—used him—just like Meno did! . . . It's no wonder the man—

APOLLODOROS *(Over the Moderator, to Phaedo)*: The last day you saw him . . . Archer . . . on the set . . . what happened that day?

PHAEDO *(Pouring herself a drink)*: We . . . were having one of *many* disagreements about how a scene should be shot . . . but this was no different than any other argument . . . the crew agreed with me . . . they usually did and that incensed Archer. He—like most men—could be bullish, had to have a certain amount of parade regarding respect in public spaces . . . we had our war of words, and we wrapped early that day. Archer and I, we . . . well, we walked around for a while . . . neither of us saying much. I tried to say something, but Archer—he was . . . he was silent. Very silent. Strangely silent.

APOLLODOROS: Did he say anything? Anything at all?

PHAEDO: We walked . . . until we came to a movie theatre. They were showing *The Four Hundred Blows* . . . He wanted to . . . see it again . . . one more time he said . . . our first time seeing it together . . . A boy and his mother. *(Her attention moves toward the Moderator)* The mother was very beautiful. The mother had betrayed the son. The son chases memory on the streets of Paris. He is arrested. He escapes. Long camera shot of boy running, perpetual running over ditches and down hills, until he comes to a beach, towards the ocean where the sand runs into an endless oasis of water. His feet have come to the edge of the earth. There is no more ground for him to run . . . He has run out of ground . . .

THE MODERATOR *(Somewhat calm, still angry)*: What did you do then? After the movie?

PHAEDO: We . . . we walked some more.

APOLLODOROS *(Prodding)*: Yes?

PHAEDO *(Drifting)*: Passed . . . *that building again . . . the old mansion.*

APOLLODOROS: And where was it?

PHAEDO: I don't remember where—

THE MODERATOR *(Sarcastically)*: You stood outside of a building—you don't remember where— *(Laughs to himself)*
Man . . . ya'll are really somethin'.

PHAEDO *(Drifting further)*: We stood there . . .

ΩΩ

APOLLODOROS: Windows shut? Doors bolted? Vanquished.

PHAEDO: Yes . . . yes, it was closed.

APOLLODOROS: Did you go in?

PHAEDO: Archer climbed the gate . . .

APOLLODOROS: It was, at one time, a fine house—yes?

PHAEDO: I suppose . . .

APOLLODOROS: Built at the turn of the century, or so—yes?

PHAEDO: Archer went in . . . I . . . waited . . . and then I went in
after him . . . it was boarded up . . .

APOLLODOROS: Heavy wrought-iron gate of leaves, frets, scal-
lops, surrounding four acres of handsomely manicured
lawn of rhododendron, ivy . . .

PHAEDO: Cherry blossom trees . . .

APOLLODOROS: A veranda of cast-iron . . .

PHAEDO: Stained glass . . .

APOLLODOROS: . . . with classical allusions?

PHAEDO: . . . yes.

APOLLODOROS: A sturdy façade with large transom windows
and projecting towers on each side entrance?

PHAEDO: Yes.

APOLLODOROS: Built in the mock-Gothic style . . . implying ancient
lineage—has the feel of classical ruins . . . inside . . .

PHAEDO: Two private elevators . . .

APOLLODOROS: Servant's quarters on the very top floor . . .

PHAEDO: Fireplaces in every room . . .

APOLLODOROS: Ornately carved in marble with considerable
skill . . . notice the undercutting of their floral friezes . . .

PHAEDO: Greek sculpture set on pedestals at every turn . . .

APOLLODOROS: One can get lost, easily, inside these walls . . . beneath these vaulted ceilings supported by strong Ionic columns . . . painted figurative roundels within the plasterwork—look up: elaborately hand-painted scenes from the *Bacchae*; young Pentheus, rebelling against tradition, waving his thyrsus from the highest branch of a fir tree, to destroy Dionysus. Agave, mother of Pentheus, her robes covered in blood, she has the head of her son impaled on her thyrsus: the cruelest, the kindest thing a mother can do for her son—to dismember him . . .

(The air clears.)

PHAEDO *(Startled backward)*: Here? . . . This is . . .

APOLLODOROS *(To the audience, a presentation)*: Commissioned, by one Sir Norman Victor, one of Britain's nouveau riche, self-made industrialists, a man of great means, a thinker and a lover of antiquities . . . After Sir Norman Victor died, this house was closed down . . . underwent years of renovation . . . opened to the public, decades later . . . as the Museum of Antiquities. Its first exhibit was also to be its last: ancient Greek pottery. Large-belly amphoras. These doors have remained closed since then—until now.

MENO: For God sakes . . . Of course this is where the museum used to be—why do you think I came? I was on the board of this museum . . . so was Diana Vreeland and—didn't everybody know?

(Space.)

CRITO: I knew.

ION: It was in the welcome packet.

PHAEDO *(Touching the walls, weeping)*: Such a . . . a cruel thing . . .

THE MODERATOR *(Indifferently)*: I don't see what's so cruel about it.

PHAEDO: Why don't you understand? He would not write . . . he was troubled!

THE MODERATOR *(Moving on)*: Ion, if you want to give your presentation now . . .

(Ion hesitates out of respect for Phaedo.)

MENO *(To Phaedo, an afterthought)*: So, is it just ironic that you and Archer came here a year before he tore the place apart or what?

PHAEDO *(Attempting to sustain herself)*: He said . . . said he didn't want to be *bothered*—the whole damn thing had imploded and . . . of course . . . I didn't understand why he would say this . . . I was hurt . . . we had made this thing—together—I didn't understand this anger coming from a man I had loved so intensely—

THE MODERATOR *(Insistently)*: Ion!

(Ion reluctantly gathers papers, approaches the podium.)

CRITO *(To the Moderator)*: LISTEN!

THE MODERATOR: I said I heard what she had to say—Ion!

PHAEDO *(Retiring into old wounds)*: Looking at me . . . as if I were the enemy . . . going on about men who had been ruined for their associations, about the realm of meanings and values, about conservative behaviorists and the populous refusal to talk about the state of the country . . . about doing SOMETHING MORE—looking at me as if I were the enemy, as if what we had done was trivial . . . was not his . . . and then . . .

THE MODERATOR *(Sudden interest)*: And then?

PHAEDO: He sat down on my bed . . . in my apartment . . . and he looked at the walls . . . again . . . touched the walls with his hands . . . trying to feel Canada Lee's finger-prints in the plaster . . . and he cried . . . his body was heaving . . . he had his arm around his face . . . so I couldn't see . . . his face . . . said . . . we're operating under this ceiling of belief that's predicated . . . on what? . . . tried to say something else . . . tried to speak softly . . . he was touching the walls . . . said he had to get out . . . outside of these walls . . . he was . . . looking down . . . I was looking up . . . at the ceiling . . . at our storyboard . . . he said . . .

THE MODERATOR *(Softening, moving toward her)*: What? He said what?

PHAEDO: He said he did not want to be trapped there—on the verge of something—like a man standing on a ledge waiting for the courage to leap.

THE MODERATOR *(Something familiar; unsure)*: What . . . what do you think he meant by that? ". . . trapped there . . . on the verge of something"?

PHAEDO *(Barely above a whisper now)*: If . . . If you want to understand Archer . . . we should focus on the films we saw together—

THE MODERATOR *(Leaning in, his body no longer his body)*: Phaedo, what do you think . . . he meant?

(Phaedo weakens at what she sees in the Moderator's face—Archer. The closeness of their bodies . . . intimacy and betrayal.)

PHAEDO: The ones that influenced his work—*Mamma Roma*. It is not one of Pasolini's greatest films but it explores clear themes of class exploitation. Class exploitation must not be taken lightly.

THE MODERATOR: ". . . like a man standing on a ledge . . ."

PHAEDO *(Trying to pull out)*: Jean-Luc Godard's *Pierrot le Fou*. 1967. Radical approach to aesthetics . . .

THE MODERATOR: ". . . waiting for the courage to leap."

PHAEDO: Godard blocks our normal expectations about story and forces us to concentrate on the process of piecing together narrative. There is something to say about how one pieces together a sequence of events—we are all too eager to think logically . . .

MENO: Not all of us.

THE MODERATOR: Phaedo, what do you think . . .

PHAEDO: We are limited . . . so limited in our thinking.

THE MODERATOR: What do you think he meant by that?

PHAEDO: It . . . it is Godard who tells us . . . not to look back . . .

THE MODERATOR: Phaedo . . .

PHAEDO: . . . Not to hope for some revival of the past . . .

THE MODERATOR: Phaedo . . .

PHAEDO: . . . less we drown.

Ω

(Meno starts laughing. The laughter slices through.)

MENO: No—I just remembered—

(Gets up from his seat, approaches the audience:)

We had worked out a bit for the show . . . well—oh, I'm terrible— *(Laughing)* The writers had come up with a bit, you know, a sketch, to parody the whole Beat thing. And we had *great* writers in those days—Jackie Mason, Woody Allen . . . I mean I wasn't gonna do it, said it was over the top, but *(Laughing)* . . . Well, here we are, about to be back from the break and he's in the green room. I don't know if he's coming back out to read or not. So we put the sketch back in. *(Laughing)* Oh God, to think of it, and I had nixed it! But Aymes was so stiff, so he went back to the green room with the director

who's trying to talk him into coming back out, see.
Meanwhile the make-up girl—oh God, the makeup
girl—and me came up with this idea. *(Laughing)* So by
the time we're back from the commercial break we had
a bongo player and a saxophonist out onstage playing
really loudly—REALLY LOUD—get it? . . . and I—

ΩΩ

(Canned studio laughter; music; Skitch Henderson.)

—So I come out in this . . . these dark sunglasses, and
this little wig, like, you know, little tight black curly wig,
and cork, and I was—cork all over my . . . like from the
death trail—and I was reading, reading from his book
out loud with . . . using . . . you know, black slang, you
know, like Kerouac would do, black slang like the old . . .
the old days . . . Café Society! —His hair, I say his hair
was buh-LAAK! And . . . oh man . . . and the bongo
player and the saxophonist, they just kept playing louder,
and I had to compete with them, see—and I go:
"Maaaaan, his mu-tha was so cooool," like that, and oh
God: "Dadio," I say, "I say his mu-tha . . . his mu-tha
saw, she saw dat his hair was buh-LAAK! Buh-Lakuh
dan buh-LAAK! Buh-Laak, buh-LAAK!" Oh it was
sooo funny! You shoulda seen the audience, everybody
was laughing, with the little wig and the sunglasses . . .
oh God, it was soooo—we killed 'em—sooo fuuu-
unnny. Well, then I introduce Aymes. And Aymes comes
out—he didn't see the skit because he was in the green
room—and so he comes out, he starts reading: "His hair
was black, blacker than black . . ." The audience . . .
everybody—oh God!—soooo funny: "His hair was
black, blacker than black . . ." Right away everybody's
on the floor—oh how they laughed—it was soooo

funny. You should've seen his face. Everybody was laughing, the audience loved it! Oh God, they ate it up!

(Music fades. Laughter fades.)

Well, anyway . . . he never did write another book . . . I forgot all about him . . . until years later . . . when he made a . . . a mess of everything.

Ω

(Meno returns to his seat. His hands are shaking. He pops a pill.)

ION: Absurd.

APOLLODOROS: To an absurd mind, reason is useless and there is nothing beyond reason . . . nothing except an unidentified woman who lies amongst the ruins on a marble floor. —How would you like to proceed, dear Moderator?

(The Moderator stands. His back against the wall, his face wet . . . eyes wide open . . .)

THE MODERATOR: I don't know . . . I . . . uh . . . I'm afraid . . .

PHAEDO: This is the body of a man we are handling. Please, let none of us mishandle him . . .

APOLLODOROS: Perhaps . . . we should recess . . . for ten minutes or so?

ION *(For Crito)*: I'd like to remind the panel that I have not delivered my paper yet . . . Marks, the protest . . .

THE MODERATOR: Yes, let us all recess.

(The panel exits. Apollodoros takes a seat.)

APOLLODOROS *(To the Moderator, stopping him before he leaves)*:
You don't remember him, do you? You have no recol-
lection of him at all?

THE MODERATOR: How . . . —No . . . of course not . . .

APOLLODOROS: You are at such a disadvantage here . . . *(Raising
her glass in a toast)* We must remember that. All of us—
when we view the body—again.

MODULE 3

Practicing Death

I'll bet everyone's asked themselves at one time or another . . . what we're here for and what God's plan is for our lives . . . and somewhere down the mental road you're walking, you start to wondering what really matters and what's just the bullshit that gets thrown up to distract you . . . are you living in some dream of your own imagination?

—SNOOP DOGG

Lights up on Ion standing at the podium. He speaks in the manner of the Sophists. **lxiv**

ION: I think it was Socrates who said, "When a man aspires for wisdom, he is already practicing dying." Practicing dying. When we speak of Archer Aymes, reflect on what we know of his life, piece together the bits of information we have, it is important that we keep in mind that we are not speaking of the process of life, but rather, the process toward death. In Aymes's process toward death, there are many turns, leaving behind trails of things to be understood in his eternal silence. I would like to give voice to the silence of Archer Aymes. Looking at the remnants of myth that was Archer Aymes, there are years we cannot account for in his life, small gaps, and dark holes. We are left some facts and many lies. The only documented facts or public records pertaining to the life and death of Archer Aymes begin with war and end with war. Who was Archer Aymes? Did he invent and stage his future in the

95

absence of creative impulses? Let us look at what we *think* we know. We know he spent some years teaching at New York University, and as I say in my biography of him: ". . . Further occupying space and expending time— teaching nothing and attempting to learn everything." From this point on, his life is rooted in meaninglessness. According to my research and interviews, Aymes *did* spend some time at The New School in the 1940s—this is a very important piece to the puzzle that is Aymes. It contradicts his own claim that he was just twenty-two or -three in 1959, and forces us to Meno's claim that Aymes was already hanging out in bars with young writers as early as 1949, or 1950—

MENO *(To the Moderator)*: I told you.

ION: And I am inclined to believe Aymes began the process of inventing himself as a postmodern Surrealist at The New School, as early as 1946, because the man who I suggest, in my biography—due out next month—the man who was his true mentor, was living in New York City in 1946. André Breton.

CRITO: Who?

ION: André Breton.

PHAEDO: This . . . this is completely ridiculous! There is no evidence whatsoever that the man was at The New School or ANYWHERE with André Breton!

ION: Excuse me—I am speaking!

PHAEDO: I've sat here and listened to this endless rambling— these silly suppositions about Archer—comparing him to Kerouac, a man who NEVER came close to achieving anything as valuable as *Mother and Son*! As for André Breton—

CRITO: Who the fuck is André Breton?

ION: Aymes taught French modernist literature at NYU, when you were there, did he not?

PHAEDO: He taught it, he was NOT influenced by it! Look at his film—his influences are CLEAR!

THE MODERATOR: Phaedo, I believe Ion has the floor—

MENO: If she wants to talk film, let's go back to Kerouac and *Pull My Daisy*.

ION: I DON'T CARE—I have the floor!

PHAEDO: I have listened—

THE MODERATOR: Phaedo—we must allow Ion—

PHAEDO: I have ALLOWED quite enough!

CRITO: He talked all through her shit!

ION: Well if I'm not going to be allowed to say what I—

THE MODERATOR: I'm going to have to ask—

PHAEDO: I have listened to quite enough about JACK KER-OUAAAAC and ANDRÉ BRETOOOON! Enough has been said—

THE MODERATOR *(Stands up, banging his fist on the table)*: PLEASE!

APOLLODOROS: Yes. Oh yes. There you go.

(Ion proceeds.)

ION: Thank you. André Breton, the great French Surrealist, came to New York in 1946, joining his fellow exiles Marcel Duchamp, Claude Lévi-Strauss and Max Ernst. I was able to locate at least one man—

PHAEDO: What man? Who?

ION: Who was a student at The New School at this time, who recalled these meetings with Breton as early as 1946, and he was sure the man known as Archer Aymes was present at these meetings. It is most probable. *(Pauses for an inevitable outburst. None. He continues)* After breaking from the Dadaists, Breton had embarked upon inventing a controversial new way of writing—automatic writing. Kerouac attempted this, and—in my opinion—failed at it—

PHAEDO: Miserably.

ION: But Aymes, to his credit with his *Mother and Son*, is the first to achieve it since Breton in the 1920s. In an inter-

view with *Playboy* magazine in 1960—one of his most
controversial interviews—Aymes, when asked if he is
influenced by Jack Kerouac, dismisses Kerouac, almost
directly quoting Breton—explaining that automatic
writing "requires the mind detach itself from the solici-
tation of the external world and from individual cares of
a utilitarian or sentimental nature . . . requires divorcing
oneself from Western thought . . . something Jack will
never be able to do."

PHAEDO *(To Apollodoros)*: Any more wine, dear?

MENO *(Under)*: Wait a minute . . .

ION *(On a roll)*: Further in this interview, Aymes uses the Surrealists to dismiss Norman Mailer's 1957 essay "The White

lxv lxvi Negro" when he points out that it was Verlaine who *first*
described Rimbaud as "the White Negro. The splendidly
civilized, carelessly civilizing savage." Aymes went on to
say: "Unlike myself, Mailer is a man in search of a movement." But Aymes *was* a man in search of a movement.

CRITO: Aymes was not a man in search of a movement; he was
a man in search of a war.

ION: I agree with you there—but the war was—

PHAEDO: He was an artist. Plain and simple—

CRITO: And he wasn't tryin' to create no movement with no
goddamned book!

ION: I'm sorry?

CRITO: Movements are not *created* by writing no motherfuck-
ing poems and publishing no goddamned poems in
books and selling them books to book buyers.

PHAEDO: Movements, when they are effective, are CREATED
by people with common challenges!

CRITO: Philosophies—politics!

PHAEDO: Socioeconomic perspectives, aesthetics—

ION: I know how movements are—

PHAEDO: And movements are not *self-consciously* created!
Movements are not *created* before the movement *discov-*

ers itself, *defines* itself and *regenerates* itself—occupying the hearts and souls of people—

ION: Right, well—

CRITO: And a movement does not fuckin' *name* itself!

PHAEDO: They're named by newspapers and TV talk-show hosts!

CRITO: And lame duck Johnny-come-lately biographers!

PHAEDO: *Dig it!*

CRITO: Because *movements* can operate *without* names and incorporations and publicity—

ION: When it's your turn, you can—

CRITO: Movements are created *before* they are recorded—

PHAEDO: Or photographed!

CRITO: Or published and introduced into the marketplace!

PHAEDO: The marketplace has *never* CREATED a movement—

CRITO: NEVER! The marketplace of hip and cool is always—

PHAEDO: ALWAYS!

CRITO: The death of movements!

ION: Well, I was suggesting—

CRITO: Go 'head then, motherfucker—

PHAEDO: SUGGEST!

CRITO: Ain't nobody stoppin' you!

MENO *(A gag)*: You know, speaking of movements—where the hell is the—

THE MODERATOR: Ion, please continue.

ION: . . . Breton, who would have, most likely shared with Aymes his method of recording dreams, interpreting dreams and free associations—was plagued by what he called a "daily fatalism." Much of Aymes's novel feels as if the man who wrote it is lamenting something *inside* himself—*and* longing to rally against something outside himself—

THE MODERATOR: Ion, what is your point? Simply that Aymes's work may have largely been inspired by Surrealism?

CRITO: And so what?

ION: Not just by Surrealism—but what Surrealism was made of! And this, which is more important, influenced more than the work—it influenced the man!

PHAEDO: IT DID NOT INFLUENCE THE MAN!

THE MODERATOR: The Surrealists were an influence on the entire post-war generation of writers and artists. This is not a secret. But Aymes, with his theory of there being no tomorrow—no art tomorrow— You're all missing the point! Didn't the man just write a book about a mother and her son?

APOLLODOROS: And ground.

THE MODERATOR: Isn't it as simple as that?

CRITO: *Nothing's* as simple as that.

THE MODERATOR *(Losing it)*: But that's the book I read! Not a book on Surrealism or Maya Deren or whatever. I mean, you miss the point—I think *I* missed the point—it's not about the mother being the earth, and the son being the artist born of the earth. The book I read is about a mother who . . . who loves her son, about a son who . . . is abandoned, feels *betrayed* by his mother. And I . . . I fell in love . . . with it because . . . that's what . . . I mean . . . it's what I'd been trying to . . . say . . . to write . . . and what do I do with that? . . . the words in my head . . . I try to put the words down . . . but I can't . . . I can't find them when I go lookin' for them. —And . . . then . . . you find a book . . . some book . . . a simple story . . . you fall in love . . . but then . . . you feel as if . . . you'd been slapped in the face . . . for falling in love with it . . . because . . . here they are—*your* words—what you were trying to say was already said . . . already done . . . and— *(Suddenly self-conscious)* Aymes said he didn't believe in his art . . . in his book, said there'd "be no art tomorrow." —What do I do with that? Huh? That's what I want to get to. I want you to help me locate a man—find *him*—help me understand what I read—

APOLLODOROS: You did not *read* Aymes—you *experienced* Aymes—that is what he intended. What you felt is exactly what he felt—you lived it as he had lived it. Do you know why he said there would "be no art tomorrow"?

THE MODERATOR: I assume . . . because . . . he was saying . . . society and the politics of society wouldn't allow it.

APOLLODOROS: No.

THE MODERATOR: Well for whatever reason he made the statement—wouldn't you say Aymes's statement was political? Wasn't he pointing us in the direction of political and social failure?

PHAEDO: Yes. He was not a Surrealist—Surrealism was concerned with poetry, dreams and the marvelous. Nothing else.

ION: Wrong. The Surrealists *were* political—this comes directly from Breton's interviews with André Parinaud—

MENO: Wait a minute—

ION: They believed in the social transformation of the world—accomplished at any point—but they never valued this above the poetry of dreams—

MENO *(Laughs)*: You're wrong—

ION: Out of which the transformation of the world would come. This was *exactly* what Aymes was constructing, after meeting Breton when he came here in 1946—but I'm ahead of myself—

MENO: You're *wrooooong* . . .

ION: What?

MENO: I met André Breton when he was here.   lxvii

ION: What?

MENO: Lived over on West 56th Street. He didn't *come* here in '46, came here with his wife in '41, gave a speech at Yale in '42, went to Canada in '44, came back to New York, wife dumped him, he left New York for good in '45—

PHAEDO: Died in Paris in '66. I wore black. No shoes. No panties.

MENO: Only time Breton ever went to The New School was in '42 to see an exhibit of Enrico Donati's . . . I have a photographic memory for detail.

(Beat.)

CRITO *(To Ion)*: Obviously, you don't know how to fact-check.

PHAEDO: Cashed the publisher's check yet, dear?

ION *(Disoriented)*: Well . . . anyway, I only brought up . . . Breton . . . as a . . . means of . . . of . . . looking at Aymes and . . . and his . . . uh . . . failure . . . at creating something new—in form. The constant failure . . .

PHAEDO: Yours! Not his!

(Beat.)

THE MODERATOR: Ion, do you need a minute?

ION *(Pressing forward)*: And . . . uh . . . though Apollodoros may not be able to answer the question as to why Aymes made his great fatalist statement about the death of tomorrow and art, I can answer that question in very plain and simple language—failure! The book. The film. The Civil Rights demonstration in Mississippi. The demonstration at the museum. The invented identity. All failures!

APOLLODOROS: Yes . . . very *plain* and very *simple* language!

CRITO: Ain't this some bullshit? Then what the fuck we doin' here if it was all failure?

PHAEDO: We are here because he was NOT a failure. You are COMPLETELY misplaced at this conference! The failure is in your placement at this—

THE MODERATOR: Ion, I can't imagine you mean this literally. Please explain—

PHAEDO: If he could explain what he meant, darling—

ION *(A comeback, notes be damned)*: The problem with the work of Aymes is that it is modeled after a European aesthetic—though he identifies himself as a black man (a Negro)—and the work is ambiguous in a way that may have served it commercially, or better said, the book inspired some commercial curiosity, but it was destined to fail because it did not reach, to borrow a phrase, "the souls of black folks." So he tried to make an obvious attempt at connecting art and politics and blackness—a REAL statement about race by joining Negro protestors. But before this protest, he'd focused on the dreams, the style of his Surrealists mentors. And he'd constructed a postmodern Negro identity for himself, but he had not been overtly Negro in style, or manner, or soul—didn't know how.

THE MODERATOR: What do you mean, he "didn't know how"?

Ω Ω

ION: Aymes did not tell Meno he was black when they met in 1950—no one knew he was black when the story came out in . . . uh . . . *Esquire*, because the writing of Aymes was void of any real ethnic stylizing. Men I've interviewed, when asked about Aymes, have said they had NO knowledge of Aymes being Negro until *after* the book was published—and even then, it was difficult for people . . . to accept because of his obvious Caucasian features—

MENO: Oh I don't know how difficult it was—everybody saw that movie with Lana Turner, *Imitation of Life*—

(Apollodoros slowly rises to her feet.)

ION: In his first printed interview—in the *Paris Review* with George Plimpton—two months before the book reaches the stands, Aymes offers that his mother is Greek and his father is Negro, and both had died. One month later, Aymes insists on rewriting the book jacket bio—identifying the birthplace of his father as Marks, Mississippi. *And* he insists on there not being an author's photo of him—at all. AND initially, the book jacket had very simple cover art . . .

THE MODERATOR: A Greek statue of a mother and her son . . . the title printed in gold against blue—

ION: But Aymes insists on using a photograph he provided the publishers with . . . an old crumpled photograph of a Negro *woman* and a little boy, their faces obscured in shadows. It is ripped in half and bonded together with yellowing tape. Despite objections from the publishers, Aymes insists this photo is used for the cover of the book—the publishers promise him they will use it . . . but they do not.

THE MODERATOR: What happened to the photo?

ION: I don't know. I think it was lost.

THE MODERATOR: The woman . . . the boy, who were they?

ION: I don't know . . . maybe it wasn't anyone Aymes knew at all—Van Doren said he thought Aymes was trying to play some game of race representation.

THE MODERATOR: Why?

(Apollodoros paces the floor. Hums. No one notices.)

ION: Because . . . I believe, Aymes was interested in . . . uh . . . adapting an ancient identity—if you will—but he would not be allowed to . . . to perform this ancient identity without meeting danger.

THE MODERATOR: What ancient identity? I don't—

ION *(Loosening his collar, pushing)*: Turn-of-the-century Bohemian culture was preoccupied with the primitive. Baudelaire identified with the outcasts of his time—

APOLLODOROS *(Out of nowhere, a field holler)*: HE HAAAAD A MULATTO LOOOOOOVER—OF ILL REPUTE!

ION: Gautier and Alexandre Dumas traveled through Spain—
APOLLODOROS *(Evangelical response)*: Weeeeearing GYPSY costumes!
ION *(Removing his jacket)*: Flaubert chose Egypt—out of his desire for a visionary alternative—something in contrast . . . to the grayish tonality of the French provincial landscape . . . developed a—
APOLLODOROS: LAAAABORED—
ION: A labored reconstruction of the—
APOLLODOROS: OTHEEEER—
ION: Of the *other* in his writing—a Westerner's stereotype of colorful—
APOLLODOROS: EXOTICISM—
ION: Picasso—he came under the influence of—
APOLLODOROS: AFRICAAAAAN ART—
ION: Yes!—Picasso said he understood what the Negro used their sculpture for—to help—to help people avoid . . . coming under the *influence*—
APOLLODOROS: Influence of spirits—
ION: To avoid the influence of spirits—to HELP them become independent!
ION *(Wholly under the influence)*: The Dadaists composed . . . illogical, simultaneous poems, contrapuntal recitatives, at what became . . . The Café Voltaire—
APOLLODOROS *(A savage dance on the table)*: Les Chante Negres!
ION: Performed in black cowls—
APOLLODOROS *(Drumming)*: And African drums!
ION: The Beats—
APOLLODOROS: The beat!
ION: Like Mailer—
MENO: Mailer wasn't a Beat!

(From here on, a preacher's cadence—handclaps and foot stomps.)

ION: Mailer said—IIIIIII SAAAAID MMMMAAAAILER SSSSAAID—UH—

APOLLODOROS: Tell 'em what he said!

ION: He said the white Negro—the essence of hip—its psychopathic brilliance IS the Negro, for THE NEGRO has been living in the margin . . . between totalitarianism, AND DEMOCRACY, for two centuries!

PHAEDO: Enough . . . enough . . . enough.

ION: Kerouac! Somebody help me say KEROUAAAAC!

APOLLODOROS: Jack!

ION: Was into Charlie Parker—

CRITO *(A reluctant amen)*: Billie Holiday—

ION: Jazz! And Ginsberg said—his book *Howl*—

APOLLODOROS: C'mon now! Help yo'self now—Yessuh!

ION *(Out of control, on his knees)*: He said—*HOOOOOWL*— was an imitation of a myth!

APOLLODOROS: Yes it was! A MYTH—

ION: A MYTH—Kerouac told him about Lester Young . . . blowing . . .

CRITO: Blowing sixty-nine successive choruses of *Lady Be Good*—yeah yeah—YOUR POINT?

ION *(Out of breath . . . calming)*: These men . . . they worshipped these Negroes . . . these Negro artists . . . as *artists* . . . BUT most importantly . . . as *Negroes* . . . because the Negro epitomized . . . some romantic . . . some exotic . . . dangerous other—the outcasts—and . . . as Mailer said . . . the Negro knew . . . life was war—

CRITO: Nothing but war!

ION: So the Negro kept for survival the art of the primitive . . . but the hipster, Mailer said, absorbed the existentialist synopsis of the Negro . . . The hipster could be considered . . . a WHITE NEGRO . . . as was—ARCHER AYMES!

Ω

(Pause. Ion comes to himself . . . looks to the panel. A non-verbal exchange of shock. He retrieves his belongings from the floor, turns to the audience, somewhat disoriented.)

Thank you.

(Ion returns to the table.)

THE MODERATOR: Are . . . are you saying—are you telling us Aymes was not black, or are you saying he did not perform his blackness as was expected of him? Or are you saying he failed at speaking to the black community?

PHAEDO: He was a multiculturalist!

ION: Well, I said that twenty minutes ago!

PHAEDO: He was speaking *OF THE* entire world *TO THE* entire world! In the book, as well as in the film—it was not about being black—his cause was MUCH broader than that!

CRITO: How broad is *broader than black*?

PHAEDO: I'm not saying—I'm responding to this ridiculousness. This is intolerable! The evidence of what he intended is in his film, and it is a multiracial cast—both black and white with no true focus on ethnicity. That he was black or biracial is of no consequence. This conference is about his work—race was not the point of the work!

ION: Aymes's failure was not only that he was most probably *not* a black man—but also that he was so heavily influenced by European traditions that he failed to consider producing art that talked *to* the black man in a language that the black man understands—

CRITO: What language is that?

THE MODERATOR: And neither did the Surrealists or the Dadaists or the Beats—

ION: And this is why I think Aymes took it all further by reinventing *himself* as authentically black—by performing that identity for the rest of his life—he wanted to get closer to what the European avant-gardists only objectified.

THE MODERATOR: If he *was* white, pretending to be black, then he *did* objectify blackness!

PHAEDO: Biographers objectify—objectify everything!

ION: The remainder of his life was a performance. He was a man in search of a character—

CRITO: I thought he was a man in search of a movement?

ION: Which is much more important than the art he produced—the art is a footnote, an abstract idea.

THE MODERATOR: It wasn't a footnote before!

PHAEDO: You miss the point of him entirely—he did not intend to abstract the idea! Or blur the lines between high art and commercial forms—OR BLATANTLY MIMIC BRETON. He believed we should be able to recognize whatever truth there was to recognize in art, if there was truth in it at all!

THE MODERATOR: When he wrote those lines about the boy standing on ground and taking a step onto nothing and falling—

PHAEDO: He was making circles—drawing very clear maps. Those circles become lines that connect us!

ION: I'm sorry—you're not making any sense.

PHAEDO: The lines between man and earth—the lines that take us all from conception to birth to learning toward a reaction to learning, toward some action in response to learning!

ION: I'm—

PHAEDO: If there is to be some circuitous pattern we've missed that connects us to the past—if the sounds of these chords, are to be understood as the lines between what is created now and what was created before—

CRITO: SHUT THE FUCK UP . . . let the man speak . . . *(To Ion)* I'm interested in where you goin' with this.

ION: Oh, yes . . . of course you are . . . Aymes wanted to fulfill the character of the Negro and he wanted to suffer as a Negro—an authentically black avant-garde postmodernist. Tried to gradually pull himself away from his white associations—which probably explains why he dumped you Phaedo—and became a Negro integrationist. But he couldn't assimilate as easily as he would have liked to, into a black culture—

THE MODERATOR: Because he wasn't black?

ION: Right! And he didn't have a black soul, had failed to purchase one with his art, that is, until he met what he probably considered to be an authentic Negro artist—Crito!

CRITO *(Laughs)*: Oh, you been readin' too many Surrealist novels.

ION: Have I? Aymes, when asked in a 1969 interview why he went down to Marks to join the Mule Train, said—

THE MODERATOR: "Because I am *from* there. A man must retrace his steps from wherever he is and return to where he is from at least once before he dies—"

CRITO: "or the remainder of his journey will be aimless."

ION: The Mule Train was halted, temporarily, between Douglasville and Atlanta, am I right Crito? And after Governor Lester Maddox ordered Georgia state troopers to block its access to an interstate highway—

CRITO: First of all, you gotta tell the people what they was tryin' to do—

ION: Sixty-seven people were arrested for unlawful protest. Archer and I were among them—

CRITO: I SAID YOU CAN'T STAND THERE—YOU GOTTA EXPLAIN. TELL THE PEOPLE WHAT THE MULE TRAIN—

ION: THE MULE TRAIN WAS MEANINGLESS, IT DIDN'T HAVE ANYTHING TO DO WITH—

CRITO *(Vehement explanation to the audience)*: Marks was an impoverished sharecropping community in the Mis-

lxxi

sissippi Delta. Dr. King had visited Marks in '67 with Ralph Abernathy . . . they visited a daycare center, and when Dr. King saw that all them little children had to eat for lunch was one apple—between them—he cried. That's when King decided there should be a protest against poverty in America—a Mule Train should originate right there, in Marks, Mississippi. But in 1968, King was assassinated—

ION: Yes, I think most of us know that by now—

CRITO: And Detroit and Watts and everywhere else was burnin' down—I mean motherfuckers was still on the TV— *Bewitched* and shit, actin' like political and economic structures didn't *exist*. *Brady Bunch* and shit, Tiny Tim gettin' married on *Johnny Carson* and shit, actin' like love and happiness was available to everybody—dig? I mean I'm talkin' about a collapse of expectations among motherfuckers—niggers like me who knew better—

ION: Excuse me, I'm trying to explain something—

CRITO: Niggers like me who was walking around with no place to go—talkin' to ghosts on park benches, questioning our own value—we was all fucked-up with *knee-a-lism*, see?

ION *(Correcting his pronunciation)*: Nihilism.

CRITO: The disease of the soul! And it ain't cured by fuckin' or falling in love or makin' money or makin' movies or breathin' fresh air. Naw, ain't cured by Jesus or Jay Krishna Murti or Buddha—but by *remembering*, like you said earlier, "subversive memory"—dig? Remembering every day, being taught new memories, gettin' addicted to memory—as addicted as you've become to *knee-a-lism*—

ION: Nihilism.

CRITO: 'Cause KNEE-A-LISM was the drug the government was passin' down to niggers like me—put it in the drinkin' water—you understand? But you get addicted to memory—engage it as a *practice*—till it generates *new* practices in your daily living, and you start remembering EVERYTHING from five minutes ago to pre-creation of the universe. Then you don't have room for no *knee-a-lism*—

ION: Nihilism.

CRITO: You may still be poor—still be black—but you'll remember WHY *(For the Moderator)* THEN YOU WON'T HATE YOURSELF. DIG? THAT'S WHAT MY *MOTHER AND SON VOLUME II* (soon as I get me a record deal) IS GONNA BE ABOUT! LIKE THEY WAS DOIN' IN FUCKIN' MULE-DRAWN WAGONS—LIKE PILGRIMS AND SHIT—REMEMBERING AND REMINDING AMERICA WHAT THE PILGRIMAGE TO THIS COUNTRY WAS SUPPOSED TO BE ABOUT!

ION: The Mule Train was headed toward Washington, D.C., where they would erect a temporary settlement called—

ION AND CRITO: Resurrection City.

CRITO: The war was on, dig? Some of us fought the war ridin' mule-drawn wagons, some of us were ready to take up guns and do whatever the hell we could to stay alive. It was a time of war—see?

ION: While you're at it, why don't you explain to the people what happened to Aymes in Douglasville—after he got arrested?

CRITO: I don't know what happened to Aymes after he got arrested.

ION: Are you positive you *don't* know?

CRITO: All I know is . . . what . . . about a year later, after he came back to New York and that stupid-ass film he won that award for didn't go nowhere— *(For Phaedo)* no offense—'cause nobody knew what the hell he was trying to say (not even *white* people), well not long after the critics got though trashin' his little movie, he organized a bunch of kids to go down to that museum in New

York and they started tearing the place up! I mean they was up there destroying art—ancient Greek art—and when I got back from Vietnam and I read that, I was like, man, now that's a protest!

MENO: Wait a minute—that's enough!

THE MODERATOR: Everyone please, we're getting ahead of ourselves . . .

MENO: You're talking about the protest at the museum? Aymes and a bunch of crazy hippies high out of their goddamned minds, destroying, DESTROYING—

THE MODERATOR: The protest, yes, I would like to ask you about the protest!

CRITO: It was a war!

MENO: Puh-lease!

CRITO: Aymes was all right with me after that.

ION: He was all right with you before that.

THE MODERATOR: The protest—in New York—can we talk about the protest? There are a lot of things I don't understand . . .

CRITO *(Sarcastically)*: Could've fooled me!

THE MODERATOR: After Aymes was arrested in Marks . . . on the Mule Train . . . how did he come to . . . I mean why did he . . . come back, and devise a protest in the museum. I don't know if I see the link?

CRITO: 'Course you don't!

THE MODERATOR: Was the protest intended to protest poverty in America? To pick up where the Mule Train left off?

APOLLODOROS: Oh no . . . he had moved on.

MENO: Made a mess of everything . . . smashing up all of those beautiful Greek vases—what a mess. I was on the board of that museum—millions of dollars lost. The man had clearly lost his mind!

ION: Well, before we go there—to the museum protest—there's something that should be explained about Marks—

CRITO: It was a time of war! That's why!

MENO: A woman was killed in that protest!

CRITO: Awww shiiiit!

MENO: An innocent bystander! Are you forgetting that? The man was responsible for a life! He was a MURDERER!

CRITO: Oh here they go again—white people talkin' 'bout murderers and shit. Don't gimme that BULLSHIT. How many lives white people been responsible for takin', motherfucker? It was WAR, baby—simple as that!

THE MODERATOR: A war about what? I don't understand that part of it because—

MENO: WHAT WAR?? Tell me, what WAR? Go outside. There's a war! Go stand in the desert and wave the flag—you'll see who the murderers are!

CRITO: How many murderers you have lunch with every goddamn day? Huh?

MENO: There was a war in the Gulf, one in Vietnam, I know about that war—

CRITO: I know about that war, too, motherfucker!

ION: You see I have a very critical piece of information regarding Marks and—

MENO: Before that, one in Korea and before that, one all over the world—yes. Do you mean any of those wars or the one we're in now? If you want to talk about war, talk about the real ones, the ones that threaten the democracy and safety of this country—the ones where people die!

CRITO: And people kill—

MENO: WITHOUT CHOICE! Jesus . . . what the hell are we doing? What the hell is this?

ION: You've got to discuss the Mule Train and what happened to him in Marks if you want to really know about New York and the museum—

MENO: You want to honor somebody dead—honor somebody who gave a shit when they were alive—Steve Allen! There's a man who worked his way up from nothing—invented a way of talking and communicating with people, made us laugh, wrote plays, recorded fifty-two albums, was married to the same woman for forty-six years—let's talk about him!—

ION: I have been trying to show you what I have documented about Marks—

MENO: Steve Allen: a producer of films—*real* films, with *stories*—best friend the average Joe ever had. The average Joe never wrote an experimental novel, or staged a protest . . . just got old . . . worked some shitty job with a bad pension plan . . . got old in some shitty apartment, waiting for a familiar voice to come on the radio or a gimmick that always made him laugh to come on TV . . . Skips from channel to channel, looking for a pretty girl to gawk at . . . pretty like girls *used* to be pretty . . . movie-star pretty . . . skips from channel to channel looking for Steve Allen with Don Knotts, and Skitch Henderson conducting the band . . . remember Jack Paar? Remember Jackie Gleason spraying soda-water down my pants? We gave a shit about life—about him, the average Joe.

CRITO: Average Joe is dead. Got killed in the war with Steve Allen.

MENO: You don't know a goddamned thing about war! . . .

CRITO: Oooh, I don't know about war . . .

MENO: You haven't lived long enough to know about war . . . you gotta live long enough . . . to know what it feels like to . . . to know that you're not afraid anymore . . . too old now . . . to be afraid . . . but it doesn't matter anymore . . . because you missed your chance . . . you could've taken that leap . . . said what you meant . . . what you *really* meant . . . but you didn't . . . you couldn't . . .

PHAEDO: So you said something else . . .

MENO: But that's not what you meant . . .

PHAEDO: And now . . . it's too late . . . you've already said it.

MENO: Next thing you know . . . you're sittin' in some shitty apartment . . . by yourself . . . and you think you've survived . . . because you're not afraid anymore . . . not afraid of anything . . .

PHAEDO: And now . . . it doesn't matter . . . it just doesn't matter . . .

MENO: That's a war . . .

(Beat.)

ION: May I finish?

THE MODERATOR: Crito . . . can we . . . can we just talk about the Mule Train . . . about you and Archer—

CRITO: Aymes joined people like me from Marks, to protest poverty!

ION: And people like you who were from Marks did not participate in the Mule Train journey.

CRITO: Fuck you, man—you said that to say what?

THE MODERATOR: Wait a minute . . .

ION: I was one of those sixty-seven people arrested in Douglasville. I was on the Mule Train in 1968. Aymes was there. Crito was NOT.

THE MODERATOR: That . . . that doesn't make any sense at all! Crito marched with Archer, he wrote about it in his liner notes and—

ION: I met Archer then. I spoke to him there . . . his sleeves were rolled up and he was trying to fix a wheel on one of the wagons or something and I approached him. I asked him if I could talk to him about the book that I carried with me in my knapsack, having heard he was in Marks. I . . . I . . . crouched down beside him—

CRITO: Fuck the poetry, man . . . So you was down there in Marks fixin' the wheel!

ION: I interviewed the man extensively in Marks! On two separate occasions!

PHAEDO: When?

CRITO: What two separate occasions? I thought there was
only *one* occasion?

ION: HELL—I BROUGHT THE MAN BACK TO NEW
YORK in '69! So don't tell me—

CRITO: You had nothing—nothing to do with his return to
New York!

ION: I had everything to do with his return to New York in
'69! I was with Aymes in Marks, all the way to Douglasville up until our confrontation with the state troopers in
'68. I was sent to a holding cell in Atlanta.

CRITO: With the rest of the white people!

ION: They kept us overnight and I got on the next train to
New York.

PHAEDO: You left the man to die in a segregated prison cell in
Douglasville! He was a celebrated writer! An American
hero!

MENO: So was Steve Allen!

ION: Oh for God sakes!

THE MODERATOR: You said . . . you said he refused to talk . . . had
given up talking . . . you said you met Archer on the
Mule Train march to Douglasville. The two of you
were arrested, spent ten months in jail. Said, "We pre-
pared for war." You went to Vietnam, he came to New
York—isn't that the story? Isn't that what you said?

PHAEDO: Over ten months, unlawfully imprisoned, dying in
that prison cell in Douglasville! And you did nothing
about it!

ION: He was not in any prison cell in Douglasville for ten
months! Or in any cell in Atlanta! Not even for one
month!

PHAEDO: He was there! He talked about it! He spoke of it!

THE MODERATOR: Lies. Lies. Lies.

ION: I'd learned his film was going to show at the film festival and still no one knew where he was. I'd read that
Aymes's film was up for the Bunuel Prize.

PHAEDO *(Under)*: There was nothing left of him when he came back

THE MODERATOR: You weren't even there!

ION: My editor was suddenly interested in the profile piece. Aymes was press-worthy again . . . Aymes had been missing for almost a year after the Douglasville incident.

THE MODERATOR: Fuckin' lies . . .

ION: So a writer friend and I took that long drive down South in an old beat-up Chevy with about forty dollars between us and lots of tape.

MENO: Cannastra . . . Pollock . . . Jack . . . Archer . . . dead . . . all dead . . .

PHAEDO *(Under)*: I watched him screaming on my television screen. The police . . . the museum . . . Archer . . .

ION: In the thirty hours or so it took us to arrive in Marks, I prayed he would be alive in some jail cell so that I could be redeemed.

CRITO: Well, at least your hands would've been clean.

THE MODERATOR: Bullshit.

ION: Listen, if I were you—

CRITO: So get to it. Where was he when you found him?

ION: You know where he was!

PHAEDO: Rotting, in a jail cell in Douglasville!

ION: He was not—

PHAEDO: TEN MONTHS CRITO WAS WITH HIM! TEN MONTHS!

THE MODERATOR: Were you even in a jail cell with the man? . . .

CRITO: We shared a cell for one night.

THE MODERATOR: Excuse me?

CRITO: It was in—uh—June of '68. I was only there one day. I was released the morning after we met and then I went . . . went to Vietnam.

ION: Are you sure about your dates, Crito?

CRITO: I'm sure about puttin' my foot up yo' ass!

ION: Let me refresh your memory.

CRITO: I said I was with the man for just one night in Douglasville in June of '68 and then I went to Vietnam.

THE MODERATOR: Said you were in a jail cell with him for three weeks, said he refused to talk . . . so he hummed . . . communicated to you by hummin' or some shit . . . and you went to Vietnam and you remembered his hummin' . . . and when you got home, you recorded his hummin' into a hand-held tape recorder and then made a chart of the music, and spent years composing it while you traveled with Wayne Shorter, until you made your first album, *Mother and Son, Volume I*. Track 1: "The Sound of Archer Aymes" . . . so that was a lie too?

CRITO: I know what the FUCK I did! I played Hammond organ, used John Faddis on trumpet, Ken Swank on drums, Bob Stewart on tuba, Jeanne Lee on vocals. Recorded in West Lake Music Studios, out in Hollywood. I was fuckin' this Swedish chick with a mole the shape of Africa on her right ass cheek. We moved to Holland three months later—dumped the bitch and came back here to start my second record. So I know where the FUCK I was and who I was with—and I KNOW MY ASS IS BLACK! YOU GOT A QUESTION?

THE MODERATOR: I'M ASKING YOU A QUESTION—

CRITO: THEN ASK ME A MOTHERFUCKIN' QUESTION—don't run the mojo DOWN on my BLACK ass with your little index cards and shit. Cuz I'll walk right the fuck out this sonuvabitch!

THE MODERATOR: Walk! Walk! I DON'T GIVE A FUCK! ALL OF YOU MOTHERFUCKERS WALK!

APOLLODOROS: Oh, yes!

PHAEDO: They must have taken Archer from Douglasville to Atlanta or somewhere in Mississippi and imprisoned him there!

ION: He was not in prison in Atlanta! He had been released from prison in Douglasville only two days after the confrontation! I should know. I found him. Crito, should I tell you where I found him?

CRITO: Don't tell me, tell him! *(Points at the Moderator)* TELL HIM where. Where did you find him, Ion? Tell him where you found Archer!

ΩΩ

ION *(Reading from his manuscript)*:

> He returned to Marks, Mississippi. He was living on a run-down pre–Civil War cotton plantation where he worked no less than ten hours a day, making no more than $2.50 for a full day's work chopping cotton. There was a woman with whom he shared a small run-down wood-framed house on the opposite end of the cotton field from the main house. A handsome Negro woman, with salt-and-pepper hair . . . the house they shared—

CRITO: Faced the main house—

ION:

> A derelict mansion of some stature solely occupied by his employer and landlord—

CRITO: An eighty-nine-year-old white Mississippi native.

ION:

> Only surviving son of a once-prominent cotton plantation owner. The five or six small cottages that lined the cotton fields, Archer's among them, were built as—

APOLLODOROS: Slave quarters no less than one hundred and twenty years before.

ION:

Negro families who had been there for generations occupied them all. As it was explained to me, they were all
descendants of slaves who had lived and worked on that
very same plantation and never left . . .

ION AND CRITO:

Even after emancipation.

ION:

I arrived. He agreed to come back . . . with my friend and
I the next morning. I didn't hear him say good-bye to the
Negro woman he lived with. I didn't hear her say good-
bye. I never heard her voice. She stood behind the screen
door . . .

APOLLODOROS: Expressionless—

ION:

. . . watching us as we pulled up to the house to collect him,
holding the door open only slightly. He emerged from behind
her in his overalls and fisherman's hat with no luggage . . .

APOLLODOROS: Walked a normal and steady pace . . .

ION:

She watched our orange Chevy devour him. Her eyes
stretched out beyond the ripped screen . . .

CRITO:

Across dense rows of brush . . .

ION:

. . . up the mile-long dirt path toward the elaborate rusting
iron fence, at what must have then become a tiny orange
dot. Neither of them waved . . .

(Closes his book) It's all in my manuscript if any of you care to read it.

THE MODERATOR: Who . . . who was the woman?

ION: I don't know. Perhaps Crito knows. You were born and raised on that plantation, yes?

CRITO: And?

ION: You are the descendant of generations of slaves and sharecroppers who have worked that plantation—yes?

THE MODERATOR: He was there—on the plantation, the entire time? The year he had been missing?

ION: Where were *you*, Crito, the year Archer was missing?

CRITO: You tell me!

ION: I don't know . . . I do know you are from Marks, Mississippi—

CRITO: Land of the tree, home of the grave!

ION: I do know that plantation was your birthplace. I do know you were first arrested in Mississippi in June of 1968. Not for unlawful protest, but for drunkenness and disorderly conduct. You did share a jail cell with Archer Aymes for one night. I DO know that you went to Vietnam from May of 1966 to March of 1968! BEFORE you returned to Marks—BEFORE you met Aymes—NOT after. You DID NOT go to Vietnam after that! That's a lie! The question is, WHY? Why did you misrepresent these facts on your *Mother and Son* album? Why did Aymes live on the plantation where you were born? That I do NOT know! Can you explain that to the panel, Crito?

CRITO: I just left Joe Henderson playing *Mind Over Matter* on the goddamned street corner—

ION: What?

CRITO: Wayne Shorter! *Schizophrenia!* Curtis Fuller on trombone, Joe Chambers on drums—I'm sayin' on my way here, tonight, in my walking . . .

THE MODERATOR: The music, a lie. The movie, a lie. The book, a lie.

CRITO: I had to step over Wayne Shorter because somebody had thrown him out of their window or put him out with the goddamned garbage. Joe Henderson—*In Pursuit of Blackness*—Pete Yellen on alto sax, Stan Clarke on bass, Lenny White on drums . . . Ron Carter and Elvin Jones . . . Misty landscapes . . . wild flowers and strange dimly seen shapes—*Infant Eyes*—

ION: If we're not going to address the matter at hand—

BROMIOS

CRITO: Richie Havens' *Stonehenge*, David Murray's *Morning Song*—layin' out in the moth-er-fuck-ing street! *Jazz at Massey Hall* (greatest jazz concert ever): Parker, Dizzy, Max, Mingus, Bud Powell, Toronto, 1953—layin' out on the curb. I don't have a goddamned thing to explain to the panel!

THE MODERATOR: I listened to that song . . . over and over . . . I listened to that song . . . read the book . . .

CRITO: Truth is . . . *MOTHER AND SON, VOLUME I* . . . truth is . . . *VOLUME I* didn't have a goddamned thing to do with nothin' Archer said in his jail cell! Not in Mississippi.

ION: Not in New York either.

CRITO: Not a GODDAMNED thing! *VOLUME II*—soon as I get me a record label—that's gonna tell the shit!

THE MODERATOR: So you were using Aymes, too?

(Pause.)

CRITO: What does it matter? Music is music. Ain't music enough? Like *art*?

THE MODERATOR: What is it ya'll want me to believe?

CRITO: I don't give a fuck what you believe! What do you want to believe?

(Beat. The Moderator seems unstable, murmurs to himself. Deconstruction. Ion focuses his attention on Crito. Crito focuses his attention on the Moderator.)

CRITO *(Over)*: Wayne Shorter asked a question once—he said, "I wonder if a young musician, hearing another musician, has an instinctive desire to compete with the other musician, or instead, *to join forces* and compare notes? And if they were to get together, and if their notes were appraised by a third party—let's call that third party the critic—would these two musicians be so influenced by what the third party says that they would strive to compete with one another in order to please the critic? In addition the third party (the critic) speaks to a fourth party—the public—and in pleasing the critic . . . do you please the public?"

ION *(Under)*: What agreement was made between the two of you? What conversation transpired? Why did he assume your life? Why did he live in your house in Marks—like Valéry, hiding out from the world, taking time to understand what the next step would be—Plato's cave. You meet Aymes, who turns his performance over to you . . . lives in your house on a plantation—an authentic Negro experience—giving you passageway to come to New York: an exchange. Multiple selves. Each self observing the life of the other . . .

PHAEDO: Moderator . . .

THE MODERATOR: CUT TO cross falls from wall; CUT TO sheets, covered in blood; CUT TO woman with a baby resting on her stomach; CUT TO various shots of his face, hands, his feet . . .

(Phaedo motions toward him.)

PHAEDO: Dear, Moderator . . . perhaps we should . . . reconvene . . . in another hundred years—
CRITO: NO! LEAVE HIM ALONE!
THE MODERATOR: CUT TO bullshit . . . bullshit . . . bullshit . . .

(Beat.)

CRITO: That's right . . . push it baby, push it . . . beyond life . . . beyond truth. Like Beethoven—creating the hero—a real emblem for hope. Beethoven's music—it didn't stop where you thought it should stop—didn't even stop where he had indicated to you it should stop. What'd you tell these people earlier? They've arrived at the end? You think *you've* arrived at the end? Yeah . . . but now you have to *wait* for the end . . . you—you haven't arrived at shit. What is the end? Where is it? What determines it? It's not based on what you know . . . it's based on what you don't know. Archer, like Beethoven, was overcoming deafness, pushing beyond his own deafness, baby—our deafness—that's what Archer was talking 'bout . . .
ION: Lovely digression—too bad it has NOTHING to do with you and Aymes exchanging lives. And then there's the whole issue about Aymes in the jail cell, before he committed suicide.
CRITO: Aymes didn't commit suicide!
ION: His body was found—
CRITO: There is no body! Did you see a body? I didn't see no body! You see the body?

MENO: Well, who's body . . . how do you explain the body in the . . . The police found a body . . . the body was identified as—

ION: What are you saying? He didn't commit suicide?

CRITO: I'm sayin' there was no body. THERE IS NO BODY!!!

ΩΩ

(Intense light isolates the Moderator.)

THE MODERATOR:

> And in morningtime, there was just peace and safety, there was just light, bursts of orange-and-red embers, light, in every corner, everything, flushed in gold and light, coming through leaded glass in morningtime, safe, and the world was a safe place without government or magistrates, safe, no dimensions, and the city was not a city, it was a mass of light, and in the center of her room flushed in gold, her infant, new, safe, and everything was safe and sweet, just light, but when the cool of afternoon descended, no light, and beyond the leaded glass, evening fell, with evening there was no light, no safety and the city was not a city but an open mouth of teeth, and the buildings were teeth, rows and rows of teeth, crowded, jagged, teeth, one huge open mouth, a face pulled back, with its cavernous pit, with its open mouth, waiting to swallow, pulled back, outside the window, waiting to chew, and the boy in her room, just a boy, still fresh, but nothing was sweet, and she was afraid . . . he would learn to walk the streets of the city, walk into the mouth, be devoured, afraid, he was not safe, afraid, and she took his head and hid it away, and he grew up and walked without a head and he walked among the teeth, without a head, walked, without, gnawed, without . . .

Ω

(The Moderator turns his attention to Apollodoros. Sudden collapse of recognition.)

ION *(Still outside of it all)*: That's not Aymes. That's not from *Mother and Son.*

APOLLODOROS *(Satisfied)*: No . . . . it isn't.

DITHYRAMB

CRITO *(Steady progression, music building under him)*: He said no words . . . no . . . more . . . words . . . I tried to write that . . . couldn't write that . . . how you write a sound? How you write a sound? No way. No possible way . . . What I set out to do was personal . . . private . . . between me and him . . . us . . . don't owe nobody no explanations about what happened between us . . . but I tried . . . tried to give it to you in music . . . everybody had a structure . . . a deadline . . . It was business! Art as bizzzz—ness! This is the way it's supposed to be done, they said . . . the way they do it . . . in *Americuh* . . . been doin' it . . . in Europe . . . but all I heard was a sound . . . and that was all it was supposed to be . . . but how you write that down? . . . all I heard was a sound . . . he made a sound . . . like this *(Makes sound)* . . . unstructured sound . . . what you gonna do with that? . . . huh? . . . tell me . . . what you gonna do with that?

(An assault—declaration of war in Pentecostal jazz riffs) They don't want nothin' like this—won't put it on the radio. What did the war say? —America eats its young! I had to make me a record . . . a record of this. I had to speak to what led up to that little ditty he hummed me in his jail cell—dee deee—like that. And it was all there—but that's *VOLUME II*! When I got . . .

finally . . . finally got . . . got my ass to New York, missing a toe and no hearing in my right ear . . . you tol' me Archer baby, you said don't be hungry, Crito, take it slow . . . say what you mean . . . but I . . . had to make me a record . . . write some music about . . . three days into the offensive . . . South Vietnamese attacking the An Quang pagoda . . . like John Lee Hooker attacked his music *Live at Soledad* . . . Hooker said come play with me . . . when I finally got my ass back, missing a toe, with one good ear . . . come play with me . . . with Luther Tucker and Charlie Grimes on guitar, at a California correctional facility . . . Hooker and them playin' that music at that prison, off Highway 101—1972, me playing keys with a toe left over there in Vietnam and one good ear. Archer, you said take it slow, Crito!—eeeasy!—they'll eat ya up, Crito, you said. But I had to play—chaotic fighting in the streets of Saigon, wounded civilians, South Vietnamese troops taking away prisoners who they said were Vietcong—John Lee Hooker *Live at Soledad*, yeah . . . like that! . . . Ken Swank on drums . . . and we didn't know when that shit would be over . . . didn't know till the guards turned off the electricity. See, guards turned off the lights and we had to stop playin'—BAM—South Vietnam's General Loan carrying out a summary execution in the streets of Saigon (rat a tat tat). And when I got home, read in the paper, Archer was in jail, baby. Archer said to me from his jail cell, said all we got now is sound . . . all we got now . . . Walter Cronkite on the TV sayin' everything was all right . . . Easy, eeeeasy, like how Lex Silver played that Fender bass for them prisoners . . . eeeasy . . . and General Loan was off the TV, and the news had settled back into its normal routine. "*Business as usual,*" Roberta Flack said . . . "business as usual." And Archer had gone and tore shit up in that museum . . . gone up in there with twenty-five or so and broke up them Greek vases 'n' shit. And Archer was in jail, said to me, all we got now is sound. The guts and glory image of the pre-Tet period was gone forever, the story had to have a happy ending, the Americans and the South Vietnamese were the good guys. Me with a missing toe and one good ear limping my way to a jail cell to see Archer, and Archer said to me, man, all we got . . . yeah . . . all we got . . . yeah! . . . is sound—no words, no words, nothin' mo' to say 'bout this shit. American motives were good—war is a national endeavor, war is an American tradition, war is manly, war is rational. John Lee Hooker say, come play with me at Soledad . . . Archer dead by then . . . my *Mother and Son, Volume I* started off with that shit! . . . And Archer, you said to me, Crito, no more language, nothin' to write about now . . . time to die . . . ba-ba-ba-ba-baaaa-dee-dee-dee, like that, time to die . . . he said . . . and I had to play it like this . . . la-la-la chord progressions of death . . . of death of a man . . . of death of art . . . of DEATH!

(Crito exits.)

Ω

ION *(Goes after him)*: But the question remains, Crito—
PHAEDO *(Resigned, eyes fixed on the Moderator)*: No it doesn't. The question does *not*—remain.

DEUS EX MACHINA

(Phaedo and Meno exit. The Moderator and Apollodoros are alone, seated at opposite ends of the table.)

APOLLODOROS: You got a sound you'd like to make?

C O D A

Compositio Membrorum

All the material making up the content of a dream
is in some way derived from experience, that is to
say, has been reproduced or remembered in the
dream . . . it may happen that a piece of material
occurs in the content of a dream which in the waking state we do not recognize as forming a part of
our knowledge or experience . . . we remember, of
course, having dreamt the thing in question, but
we cannot remember whether or when we experienced it in real life . . .   —SIGMUND FREUD

Woke up today . . . surprised myself, stray bullets
poppin inside me like radiated icicles—dreamin this
was the day body would finally loosen up enough so
real me could go on about my buisness . . .
                                        —TISH BENSON

I think I may have already rehearsed the scene
which you ask me to describe . . .   —APOLLODOROS

APOLLODOROS (*Circling the table with the book*): Will you concede, dear Moderator, that all has been said and there is nothing more to say?

THE MODERATOR: . . . No.

APOLLODOROS: Do you think you understand now—have an understanding? Perhaps you think you understand?

THE MODERATOR: No.

APOLLODOROS: Would you say all has been done and there is nothing more to do, so one of us, some of us—all of us—must now therefore take our place amongst the ruins?

THE MODERATOR: No.

APOLLODOROS (*Authoritatively*): Then by all means, proceed until you *know* it.

(*She places the book in front of him.*)

THE MODERATOR (*Attempts to stand; opens the book, reads—a maternal ritual*):

> . . . He had learned that the plain beneath him now was
> ground . . . because she had giggled softly behind his ears

and repeated the word—ground—and as long as he could hear it he could sense it, and he could trust it not to fail him—ground—because he could trust her to say it . . . and she had never failed him.

APOLLODOROS *(Gentle prodding)*:
    And when he learned to walk, after she had taught him to—

THE MODERATOR:
    He learned to trust.

APOLLODOROS:
    He learned it . . . he *learned* it—

THE MODERATOR *(Closes the book; reciting from memory—first steps)*:
    He learned it by trusting the woman behind him and the ground beneath him and his remarkable ability to balance himself on it. It was remarkable to him, and it was marvelous to her, it was a marvelously remarkable thing—to him and to her . . . his ability . . . to stand, to propel himself forward. Ground . . . it was endless. As endless as his desire to walk and see—

APOLLODOROS:
    Until he came to the edge of it. The edge of what had ceased to be.

THE MODERATOR *(Proceeding toward her)*:
    He did not know there was an edge or a place that would cease to be.

APOLLODOROS *(Outstretched arms)*:
    She had not taught him that. She had not taught him that things end . . . perhaps because . . . he was too young to learn that.

(Pause.)

THE MODERATOR *(Balance)*:

But he was old enough to know that the ground was there for him and he was old enough to know how to travel it with his walking and he had even learned that there were things to be seen in the duration of his walking. Things existed at different points, at different intervals, and these were things to see, to taste, to touch, to meet. But now he balanced himself on the edge of what had ceased to be.

APOLLODOROS:

She looked away, only for a moment—to see something else—and he . . .

THE MODERATOR *(Proceeding toward her)*:

He stepped once more with curiosity and excitement— lifted his limb . . .

APOLLODOROS:

As he had learned to

THE MODERATOR:

And propelled his foot and body forward

APOLLODOROS:

As she had taught him to

THE MODERATOR:

And pushed off the ground with his hind foot

APOLLODOROS:

Propelled himself forward

THE MODERATOR:

> To see what else there was to see—and she looked
> away—and he . . .

APOLLODOROS:

> She looked away—only for a moment—and he . . .

THE MODERATOR *(Collapsing)*:

> He fell!

APOLLODOROS *(Catching him)*: Because? Because?

THE MODERATOR:

> Because . . . because he had been standing there on the
> edge of what had ceased to be . . .

APOLLODOROS: And beyond it?

THE MODERATOR *(Angry departure)*:

> Nothing firm! Nothing sure! Nothing he could trust!
> Nothing he already knew! He broke! He bled! He cried!

APOLLODOROS: They both did!

(Rest.)

So many pieces to put back together again. So many . . .
dear Moderator . . . So many pieces—a mystery but
real. There is a son. There is a mother. And there was a
woman who died—there was a man who killed himself.
Was the man the son—the one who took his own life?
Was the mother the one who died unidentified in the
halls of great antiquity? The one who fell to her death,
from the upper balcony? Did she arrive, young and

eighteen—an eighteen-year-old goddess—in a raincoat with a scarf on her head, carrying with her the words of Albert Camus? Or was she not eighteen, perhaps older . . . ancient? An ancient performance . . . the mother who had betrayed the son? Did she think to herself, perhaps, it is better to die now, for the life of my son? Perhaps it is better to die. Did she arrive at the museum . . . ailing . . . her fingers tracing a large amphora? Did it tip over? Was it the first to smash against an absolute black marble floor? Did she vanish amongst the crowd—catch a glimpse of her son there amongst the protestors, intending to destroy antiquity, things that are aged, that are of before? Did she then say to him, if it is antiquity that must be destroyed in order for you to have a voice, then let *me* be that sacrifice . . . let me? Did she climb the stone steps toward the balcony, then . . . lean against the marble railing and hurl herself down . . . onto an absolute black marble floor? Did she? Did the son observe her body, there amongst the crowd of police and protestors—his mother—lying there? . . . Did he, the son, gaze upon her and think to himself, first she had failed him . . . but now it was he who had failed her . . . because it was not his intention that she die . . . rather it was his intention to *live*? Did he take her body with him, then? Did he take her body with him wherever he went? Had he always? Did he see her body in everybody? Did he take his own life out of guilt, then? Did she have life then? Could she continue his life then? Did she rise up from the dead and give birth to him again? Has she been waiting all these years, just to give birth to him again?

(*Escorting him around the room*) We sat in a circle, Aymes, the others who crowded a small apartment. We sat in a circle, the tips of our fingers touching . . . we were silent until the dreams came . . . until prophecies or truth or dreams came . . . and about that hour when the sun lets loose its light to warm the earth, one stood up, stood up and gave a great cry to waken the others from their sleep—a caterwaul—and they crowned their heads with leaves of ivy, went out into the city, walked into the street this way . . . all silent . . . returned to the place of our beginnings . . . silent. It was ritual. Ritualistic theatre—and Archer was a man in search of a means of articulation. Visualize that moment, if you will, when he walked into the museum . . . walked pass the head of Dionysus, and the clock turret . . . the museum shop that sold replicated antiquities . . . Archer looked around him, in a trance-like state—it was a dream—and he walked through a stone vault . . . walked through two low circular pillars . . . walked through a medieval doorway built in the days of Homer . . . walked through the thickness of the wall . . . looked up toward a stone spiral staircase leading to the second floor.

THE MODERATOR: . . . She was there.

(Apollodoros walks toward the balcony.)

APOLLODOROS: She ascended to a high place . . . he saw her . . . he knew what she was about to do . . . and why she must do it . . . and Archer took a hatchet to the room of ancient Greek vases, swung with mighty force, SWUNG again with a mighty force, and there were, by then, people who screamed and yelled out, police and crowds of pedestrians running, and Archer SWUNG until pieces of clay, ancient and classic, shattered to the floor—it was a dream—and she looked to him from the balcony . . . standing there in the middle of an ancient room, surrounded by ancient artifacts . . . surrounded . . . and she called out to him: "Archer? Archer . . . what is it you want to do—what is it you are you trying to do?"

THE MODERATOR *(Becoming Aymes)*: I'm . . . I'm trying . . . trying
. . . to make something . . . something outside of myself.

APOLLODOROS: And by that you mean—

THE MODERATOR: There is a mother . . . and there is a son—

APOLLODOROS: What are they? Who are they?

THE MODERATOR: She comes to build herself a dream. She's giving birth on an open plain, undefined—her son—he's
responding to the world . . .

APOLLODOROS: YES?

THE MODERATOR: But the mistake, THE MISTAKE HE
MAKES—I make—is believing that he . . . me . . . that
I have the POWER OF RESPONSE . . . that the
WORLD WILL RESPOND TO ME!!

APOLLODOROS: What do we know—WHAT DO WE KNOW,
ARCHER?

THE MODERATOR: We know . . . we know space . . . we know
time . . .

APOLLODOROS: What space? What time?

THE MODERATOR: We know the space and time in which we
live . . . but not the outcome of it . . . we know but we
don't know—

APOLLODOROS: We know there is an ending.

THE MODERATOR: We know there is an ending . . .

APOLLODOROS: And we know there is a beginning.

THE MODERATOR: Everything to know—nothing to know—and
LIES! LIES! LIES! LIES! *(Smashes an amphora onto the
floor)* SHE STOOD THERE—on that railing—LOOK-
ING, LOOKING AT ME—

APOLLODOROS: The mother is an old idea . . . the son is a new
idea.

THE MODERATOR: And you knew . . . that I was being lied to—
LIED TO—about there being the slightest POSSIBIL-
ITY . . . of making art. And they packaged it and put a
bow around it and—TAKE IT . . . RUN . . . RUN . . .
RUN . . . NOTHING . . . NOTHING . . . NOTHING.

SPARAGMOS

APOLLODOROS: There comes a time in your life, when you discover an emptiness. You have no thought of yourself as empty. You have no thought of yourself as empty and you have been operating as if you were not. But a day comes when you are made aware of it—your emptiness—and you yearn to be full. The pain of discovering this emptiness is unequaled by anything, except the pain of this yearning to be full. That is when you begin, for the first time in your life—for the first time *with* your life—to search for a language. A tongue. A voice. A means of articulation . . .

THE MODERATOR *(From the floor)*: Nothing . . . nothing . . . nothing.

APOLLODOROS *(An old song, spoken softly)*:
    Die now . . . won't have to die no more . . .

THE MODERATOR:
    Die now . . . won't have to die no more . . .

APOLLODOROS: He sang it . . . like in the old church songs.

THE MODERATOR:
    Die now . . . won't have to die no more . . .

APOLLODOROS: He saw her.

THE MODERATOR:
    Die . . . die . . .

APOLLODOROS: He did not know her . . . but he loved her.

THE MODERATOR:
    Die.

APOLLODOROS: She leaned over the railing . . .

THE MODERATOR:

> Die . . . die . . . now . . . won't . . . no . . . more . . . die . . .
> die more . . . die . . . no more.

(Lights fade on Apollodoros.)

THE MODERATOR *(A eulogy, book closed)*:

> The room was white. A white room with a bed, an ordi-
> nary bed with white linens. A white room that smelled of
> dissolve. The dissolve of the body when beauty is less
> than memory . . . She did not look at him once but she saw
> all of him in her seeing. She looked directly at him, saw all
> of him . . . he strung sentences together—kept filling
> silence with sound . . . a sigh . . . a soft giggle . . . And he
> thought to himself this is a good thing that I should do, to
> make sounds of assurance. To make assuring sounds,
> proving to her that he was young and he was strong and
> he would always be here. Proving, rather, to himself, that
> he was young and strong and would always be here. But
> he did not want to always be here. Here smelled of dis-
> solve . . . of beauty when it is less than memory. It is bet-
> ter to promise to be young, to be strong and to always be
> there. But where is there? There was so far off. Still, wher-
> ever there is, there is where he would rather be. Not here.
> But what assurance would she have if he promised to
> always be there? Better to promise to always be here . . .
> for now.

(Fade to black.)

END OF CONFERENCE

ENDNOTES

i The Moderator describes the original idea for the cover of Archer Aymes's *Mother and Son*, but the book he holds is a copy of the first edition; the title embossed in gold letters on a blue background. (See Ion's description in Module 3, beginnning on page 103.)

ii Márquez's first novella, published in 1955 (in Spanish) as *La Hojarasca* and translated in English by Gregory Rabassa: Harper & Row, 1972. Set in the mythical village of Macondo, alternating perspectives tell the story of a man who must fulfill an old promise. Employing magical realism, key characters and events appear and disappear without warning.

iii A review of *Leaf Storm* by V. S. Pritchett, published in the *New Statesman*.

iv Socratic nature: Rhapsode, expert critic of Homer. Bacchanalian nature: Teiresias, blind prophet of Thebes.

v Socratic nature: Lover and student of Socrates; love in the hour of death . . . the ultimate object of love is the vision of absolute beauty. Bacchanalian nature: Agave, the essence of regret; a mother's betrayal.

vi Socratic nature: Virtue? Piety? Courage? A cross-examination. Bacchanalian nature: Cadmus; elderly patriarch.

vii Socratic nature: An old friend speaking the imprisoned language of mortality; one who commits small acts of injustice. Bacchanalian nature: The messenger.

viii Socratic nature: The bard speaks from passion rather than intellect; a narrator of knowledge. Bacchanalian nature: Dionysus; god of letting go, a liberator from the constrictions and restraints of ordinary life. God of tradition . . . god of the recyclical, who causes the loss of individual identity in the uncontrollable chaotic eruption of ritualistic possession; offering a surrender of self which can lead to the ecstasy of freedom or the tragedy of madness. (See introduction to *Bakkai*, translated by Reginald Gibbons and Charles Segal, Oxford University Press, New York, 2001.)

ix Though it is widely believed Ed Sullivan introduced Elvis Presley to America, Presley actually made his first television appearance on the Dorsey Brothers' *CBS Stage Show* in January of 1956, and appeared on several other television shows (Milton Berle, Steve Allen) before making his most famous appearance on Ed Sullivan's show in September of 1956.

x A thirteen-part series on CBS (in kinescope: film made for live television before videotape) in the tradition of several popular jazz music shows on television in the 1950s, including *Stars of Jazz*, *Art Ford's Jazz Party* and CBS's *The Sound of Jazz* (which featured Billie Holiday with Lester Young and Mal Waldron). *The Subject Is Jazz* featured performances by several notable musicians, including Buck Clayton, Lee Konitz and Duke Ellington. Gilbert Seldes (1893–1970) was a Harvard-educated arts critic, playwright, novelist, editor and the first director of CBS News, and is considered by many to have been the first American intellectual to legitimize popular culture, insisting in his 1924 book, *The Seven Lively Arts*, that vaudeville, musical revues, movies and jazz should be taken as seriously as the ballet or opera. He also worried about the negative effects of mass media on the quality of the arts. (See *The Lively Arts: Gilbert Seldes and The Transformation of Cultural Criticism in the United States* by Micheal Kammen, Oxford University Press, New York, 1996.)

xi *The Steve Allen Show* premiered on NBC in 1953 and is considered to be the first television talk show. On one of his most famous episodes, he introduced the controversial Beat writer, Jack Kerouac.

xii Made famous by Lily Ann Carol in 1956, Quincy Jones arranger and conductor, on the Mercury label. Carol was a big-band standup vocalist with Louis Prima and Charley Ventura.

xiii ". . . who sang out of their windows in despair, fell out of the subway window . . ." from *Howl* by Allen Ginsberg, City Lights Books, San Francisco, 1956.

xiv A known Beat Generation trendsetter between 1948–1950. His decadent homoerotic parties were frequented by Jack Kerouac, Tennessee Williams, Alfred Leslie, Allen Ginsberg and W. H. Auden, among others. Kerouac admitted to having participated in several orgies with Cannastra and to having once been sexually involved with him as well. Bill Cannastra's sudden death is said to have inspired some of the most profound American literature produced in the postwar era.

xv Undergraduate teacher at Columbia University who prompted both Alfred Kazin (a literary agent and teacher at The New School) and Robert Giroux (editor-in-chief at Harcourt and Brace) to publish Jack Kerouac's first novel, *The Town and the City*.

xvi It is unlikely that Gore Vidal would have met Archer Aymes at a party at Bill Cannastra's in 1950. In his autobiography, *Palimpsest: A Memoir* (Penguin Books, New York, 1995), Vidal makes no mention of Cannastra. In 1950, after living abroad for several years, Vidal had just returned to New York and purchased a mansion on the Hudson. Having published four novels (not two, as Ellis Amburn suggests in *Subterranean Kerouac*, St. Martin's Press, New York, 1998), Vidal was a famous best-selling author by the age of twenty-four and not a frequent guest at early Beat parties. Vidal would not meet Allen Ginsberg until 1959 at a book party for Jack Kerouac. Vidal was, however, first introduced to Kerouac by Robert Giroux at the Metropolitan Opera House in the spring of 1949, just after Kerouac had signed his first book deal, but a year before it was to be published. They would not meet again until the summer of 1953 when Vidal claims to have had sex with Kerouac in a room at The Chelsea Hotel following a night of heavy drinking with William Burroughs at the San Remo.

xvii From the early nineteenth century until the 1950s, the midwest section of Manhattan (between 23rd Street and 42nd Street) was known as the Tenderloin, and the Upper West Side of Manhattan (between 60th Street and 64th Street, west of 6th Avenue) was nicknamed San Juan Hill. Both were populated by an increasing number of blacks and Latinos. The Amsterdam Housing Project, built in the 1950s remains populated almost entirely by poor blacks and Latinos. Lincoln Center for the Performing Arts, built by city planner Robert Moses, brought urban renewal to the neighborhood he designated "a slum." The entire neighborhood was raised, and tens of thousands of its residents were relocated. The movie, *West Side Story*, was filmed on location just after San Juan Hill had been evacuated, and shortly before the area was flattened. (See Robert A. Caro's biography of Robert Moses: *The Power Broker*, Random House, New York, 1975.)

xviii The painter, Nell Blaine, often attended parties at Cannastra's and introduced Jackson Pollack to Jack Kerouac. Several years later, in a letter to Alfred Leslie (just after the publishing of Archer Aymes's *Mother and Son*), Blaine wrote: "Is this new writer, Archer Aymes, the same kid Pollack stumbled in with that night at Auden's on Cornelia Street . . . the one he met at Bill's, but he didn't even know his name and we all kept making jokes about it till Pollack took it too far?"

xix Pasternak lived in Peredelkino, Russia, until his death in 1960 at the age of seventy.

xx The gallery was founded in 1950 by Tibor de Nagy, a Hungarian banker, and his partner John Bernard Meyers, a flamboyant Irish-American homosexual, formerly managing editor of the surrealist magazine the *View* (with Charles Henri Ford) and a huge influence on the Abstract Expressionist movement and The New York School poetry movement. Myers published chapbooks, produced avant-garde plays by poets with set designs by painters, administered the Ingram Merrill Awards and encouraged the burgeoning American avant-garde movement. Though his aesthetic is said to have been reliant upon the advice of the art critic, Clement Greenberg and painter Willem de Kooning, Myers was controversial for exhibiting the figurative paintings of Fairfield Porter, Larry Rivers and Nell Blaine during the height of Abstract Expressionism.

xxi A former editor of the *View*, a Surrealist magazine in the 1940s, Myers was a lover of both poetry and painting, and invented the moniker "New York School of Poets" as a counterpart to the Abstract Expressionists. The Tibor de Nagy Gallery is named after his partner, a Hungarian banker.

xxii The great dictator of Abstract Expressionism.

xxiii A broadside first published in the early 1950s.

xxiv The possible influence of Nabokov's work on Aymes was written about by Howard Moss in his essay, "Old and New; European Influences in the American Literary Tradition" (*New Yorker*, 1961). Moss wrote: ". . . for example, the incongruent poetics and coded metaphors of Archer Aymes's *Mother and Son* bring to mind the Russian literary tradition of the elegiac autobiography, best illustrated in the works of Vladimir Nabokov." Vladimir Nabokov's first novel *Mary* was published in Russia in 1925, receiving little attention. He continued to write, publishing the novels *King, Queen, Knave* in 1928 and *The Defense* in 1930. He soon developed a Russian and French reader base that hailed his genius. The eruption of the war caused him to flee Paris for New York in 1940. *Lolita* is his most popular novel, but the book he considered to be his best work was published in 1969—*Ada or Ardor: A Family Chronicle*. Nabokov was famously shy and described himself as a "social cripple." He rarely gave interviews and avoided publicity at all costs, however, before leaving the U.S. (where he lived for twenty years) in 1961, Nabokov was asked by a reporter what he thought of Archer Aymes's *Mother and Son*. Nabokov replied: "I read it. I liked it. It is good."

xxv Largely forgotten as a writer, Robert M. Coates was one of the experimental American expatriate writers who lived in and around Paris during the 1920s, and his work was influenced by his association with such writers as Gertrude Stein, James Thurber and Malcolm Cowley. His novel, *The Eater of Darkness* (1926), is said to be the first Dadaist novel written in English. In 1929, he joined the staff of the *New Yorker*, and for more than thirty years wrote art criticism and book reviews.

xxvi It is unlikely the story was published in the *New Yorker* in the late 1950s.

xxvii It is possible the story was published in *Esquire*. In the late 1950s, *Esquire* had gained a reputation for publishing the best of the new "urban" writers such as Norman Mailer, Truman Capote, James Baldwin, etc.

xxviii An African-American pornographic magazine, not available in 1959.

xxix There is no record of Jean Genet having spoken highly of Archer Aymes's novel in 1959. However, Simone de Beauvoir mentioned Aymes in an interview regarding her 1959 memoir, *Memoirs of a Dutiful Daughter*, when she claimed that she, as well as Sartre, were deeply impressed with the new American novella *Mother and Son*.

xxx Jean Genet did not come to the United States until 1968, when he entered illegally via Canada and covered the Democratic National Convention for *Esquire* magazine, and again in 1970 when he toured college campuses in support of the Black Panther Party. The only known connection between Genet and Archer Aymes comes from former Black Panther Party member, Assata Shakur (now an expatriate living in Cuba), who claimed Genet was inspired to write the introduction to George Jackson's prison letters *Soledad Brother* (Lawrence Hill Books, Chicago, 1970), because he'd heard of Archer Aymes's death in prison earlier that year and knew George would die at the hands of the man, too— just like Archer. Jackson was murdered in his cell ten months later. According to Genet's lover, Mohammed El katrani, Genet gave his only copy of *Mother and Son* to François Mitterrand, France's socialist candidate for president, as a gift in 1974.

xxxi There is no record of Meno attributing the quote to Aymes.

xxxii Clay Felker was best known for founding and leading *New York* magazine in the 1960s, he also was a reporter and editor at *Life* and *Esquire* in their heyday of the 1950s and 1960s. He was editor and publisher of *Esquire* from 1978 to 1981, and edited the *Village Voice*, among other publications.

xxxiii Joe Fox was also Ralph Ellison's editor at Random House.

xxxiv Deren was a Trotskyite and a former National Secretary of the Young People's Socialist League of the 1930s. In 1937, she addressed a group of predominately male Socialist Party members with a controversial analysis of the USSR, citing Russia as a model for "feudal industrialism." In the 1959 letter to the *Village Voice*, Deren said Aymes's *Mother and Son* was one of the "few books written by men in ritualistic form, creating a depersonalized diagram of the maternal figure as a means of getting to the whole of the maternal character, thereby accessing the larger meaning regarding the relationship between mother and male offspring."

xxxv In a 1986 interview with Robert Wilson held at The Kitchen in New York, Phaedo spoke of Aymes's artistic process and their approach to film: "There were many important influences in making Archer's film. I'd have to say the two most important were . . . uh . . . Dudley Murphy and . . . uh . . . Fernand Léger's *Ballet Mécanique*. It's a silent film made in 1924, and it was one of the earliest films to explore film as art and artifact—not as natural object. Léger was a painter see, which is why I think the best art is made by artists who don't know anything at all about the mediums they're working in, because they're using their primary medium to influence the project at hand . . . But anyway, Léger developed his own style of Cubism and had this deep interest in machine parts—which is really interesting if you consider the fact that people expect a ballet to be a dance with a bunch of skinny girls and boys in tights and tutus—but he shows us dance from

machines, even though few of the objects in the film are actually machines, which means, Léger was painting portraits of machinations, and making these gestures dance by juxtaposing them: a woman batting her eyes, a hat, bottles—all part of the ballet. Basically, it was a series of images that played with the viewer's sense of sequence and order and progression—of what will happen next."

xxxvi See Coda.

xxxvii Apollodoros refers to Billie Holiday's final public performance on May 25th 1959, at a benefit for the Phoenix Theater in New York. Steve Allen hosted, and later commented that Holiday was "looking forty years older . . . sang terribly . . . her voice was all scratchy, no vitality, no volume, nothing." In Steve Allen's 1961 book *Mark It and Strike It*, he further elaborated, saying he'd suggested to a drooling Holiday in her dressing-room that she "lie down," to which she replied, "No, I don't want to do that. When you do that, you *die*." Holiday collapsed in her apartment six days later. (See *Billie Holiday: Wishing on the Moon*, Donald Clarke, Da Capo Press, Cambridge, MA, 2000.)

xxxviii Hentoff's inclusion of James Schuyler on a panel with Norman Mailer may have been controversial because, like Mailer, Schuyler was prone to outbursts, and nervous breakdowns. Unlike Mailer, however, Schuyler was not a prominent writer at the time. Though he was one of the New York School Poets, he would not publish poetry until 1969, and would not become known for his poetry until his Pulitzer Prize–winning collection, *The Morning of the Poem*, was published in 1979. By 1959, however, he had published his first novel *Alfred and Guinevere*. The book was not favorably reviewed in the *New York Times Book Review*.

xxxix Arthur M. Schlesinger, Jr. was film critic and historian during the Kennedy administration.

xl It has never been confirmed whether or not Aymes and Bodenheim ever met, but questions regarding Archer Aymes's personal knowledge of Maxwell Bodenheim have been raised by some. Maxwell Bodenheim, once the handsome Titian-haired blue-eyed Mississippi-born avant-garde poet laureate of 1920s Greenwich Village Bohemia, was famous for his prolific literary output which included ten volumes of poetry (William Carlos Williams anointed him the "Isaiah of Butterflies") and thirteen novels, including the bestselling *Replenishing Jessica* (1925), a raunchy tale of a young girl's sexual exploration of the Bohemian underground. The novel catapulted him to overnight fame with its Henry Miller-esque prose (deemed by many to be pornographic) and the unsuccessful obscenity trial it inspired. In the jazz age, Bodenheim was equally as famous for his noteworthy inner circle of friends (Ben Hecht, among others), as he was for his reputation for bad hygiene, petty theft, alcoholism and adulterous affairs (prompting the suicides and attempted suicides of several young women during the roaring '20s). By the 1950s, however, Bodenheim had become an aging homeless drunk and Bowery panhandler who hustled booze money, pretending to be blind, or by selling other people's poems (as his own) on the street. He was a known regular at the San Remo, a popular Greenwich Village watering hole frequented by a new crop of famous and soon-to-be-famous writers and artists (Kerouac, Ginsberg, Pollock, de Kooning, among others). If we are to believe Meno's claim that Aymes was hanging out at Bill Cannastra's as early as 1950, it is possible that Aymes also frequented the San Remo. Fueling the argument for a connection between Aymes and Bodenheim is his brief but taut mention of Bodenheim's controversial 1930 novel, *Naked on Roller Skates*. In a 1959 interview published in the *New York Age* (an African-American periodical), Aymes called Bodenheim "just another character, deservedly forgotten" and cited Bodenheim's novel of Negroes and sex in Harlem: "One of too many pornographic novels about colored people written by sexually deranged white people."

xli There are several versions of Bodenheim's murder. On a particularly cold night in February 1954, Bodenheim (by then age sixty-two and homeless) and Ruth Fagan (a woman more than thirty years his junior, whom he introduced as his third "wife," described by those who knew her as a "very attractive University of Michigan honors graduate and *Newsweek* journalist turned promiscuous Bohemian) accepted (or hustled) an invitation to share a room for the night with Harold Weinberg, a twenty-five-year-old schizophrenic dishwasher, who lived in a run-down cold-water flat at 97 Third Avenue. Bodenheim knew Weinberg from the local bars, and Fagan had established a mutually flirta-tious relationship with him, even though she had been warned by locals that he was prone to violence. The exact circumstances of the Bodenheim/Fagan murder are still murky, but the day after Weinberg escorted the couple to the flophouse where he lived, police broke into Weinberg's blood-and-wine-soaked room and discovered Bodenheim's body sitting upright on a small cot with a bullet-riddled copy of Rachel Carson's *The Sea Around Us* against his chest, two bullets in his heart, a pen in his hand and several unfinished poems scrawled on a notepad in his lap. Nearby, his handwritten "I Am Blind" sign, and Ruth Fagan's partially nude body, crumpled on the floor, stabbed several times with a hunting knife. Weinberg cheerfully confessed to the double homicide, but was found mentally incompetent and unable to stand trial.

xlii See "When Kafka Was the Rage," Anatole Broyard.

xliii Amiri Baraka.

xliv The death trail: common term for the low-end vaudeville houses or tent shows across America, usually in poor or working-class neighborhoods, Negro slums or mining camps. There was little money to be made and it was not uncommon for the shows to be racially integrated. Al Jolson is said to have toured the death trail with Bert Williams.

xlv Father of Agave, formerly the head of the ruling house of Thebes. He had no sons.

xlvi Son of Agave, grandson of Cadmus, ruler of Thebes, young moralist and anarchical warrior who sought to abolish the wor-ship of Dionysus and its hedonistic practices.

xlvii According to an interview with Jonas Mekas in *New American Film* magazine, March 1977, issue XII, the official version of *Mother and Son* submitted to the Avant-Garde Film Festival in

1968 was about "ninety minutes or so with text taken from Aymes's novel used as narration in the voice of the Mother, achieving a subjectivity of the character's psychological and spiritual evolution throughout the course of her relationship with the Son." Mekas further claimed that "the music of Erik Satie was employed as a score, which made many people think, at the time, that Aymes was imitating Truffaut, who had Georges Delerue compose original music for *Les Quatre Cent Coup* in the style of Satie and Debussey." The feature-length version of *Mother and Son* is widely believed to be lost.

xlviii Filmmaker, writer, ethnographer, Maya Deren, born Eleanora Derenkowsky in the Ukraine, is widely known as one of the founders of American independent film, and had a huge influence on the postwar avant-garde. Unlike many of her contemporaries, however, Deren denounced surrealism and documentary filmmaking as self-indulgent and inartistic.

xlix In Deren's film, several women on a beach (all played by Deren) watch one woman (also Deren) running past them.

l Phaedo's acting debut: *Outremer*, 1960, directed by Philippe de Broca, with a script by Jean-Luc Godard, produced by Georges de Beauregard, filmed in Paris, tells the story of Athenias, official mistress to Louis XIV. In a 1973 French *Vogue* interview conducted by film director Jean Eustache (recipient of that year's Cannes Film Festival's Fipresci Prize for *The Mother and the Whore*, which he admits was somewhat influenced by Aymes's film), Phaedo is asked about the beginnings of her career as an actress in France, her introduction to and subsequent relationship with Archer Aymes. She is quoted as saying: "I'd met the photographer Jean-Loup Sieff in Paris. He photographed me and sold it to a fashion magazine. Many people saw the photograph, and soon I met Truffaut and the others. I was sought after by many film directors . . . but after *Outremer* I returned to the States to attend film school. I met Archer at NYU where he was teaching—we were quite taken with each other, Archer would escort me, or rather, I would drag him to parties at either Claes Oldenburg's place or Ondine's, wherever Lou Reed and Viva were dropping acid.

Truman Capote was at this one party. Archer and Truman were casual acquaintances. Capote pretended not to remember who Archer was, and Archer was deeply insulted, so he said something insulting to Capote and Capote hurled himself to the floor, making a whole scene out of it. It wasn't long after that we decided to make a film—'something real' Archer said. But then he started doubting himself. 'It's all a trap,' he said . . . Greece—Island of the Aegean Sea, Coast of Asia Minor, Babylon to the east, Hollywood to the south. We had to let him have this collapse, we believed—in him."

li Canada Lee, a well-known African-American theatre and film actor, was to be the first African-American actor to star in a film version of *Othello* before he died. His demise is largely contributed to the McCarthy era and Lee's alleged association with Communist party members. 235 West 4th Street (where Lee died on May 8th 1952) was not far away from where Aymes lived, the seedy Marlton Hotel on West 8th Street.

lii Anne Gillain, teacher of film and literature in the French Department at Wellesley College, is the author of a critical study of François Truffaut's films and a collection of his interviews. In her essay, "The Script of Delinquency," she points to D. W. Winnicott's theories on antisocial behaviors and his concept of transitional space, as published in *Jeu et réalité* (Gallimard, Paris, 1975). Gillain claims that the adolescent protagonist of Truffaut's films "attempts to recapture, after the breakdown of his environment, the transitional space of communication, creativity and shared experience."

liii Ibid.

liv Ibid.

lv Ray Carney, considered to be one of the world's leading authorities on independent film and American art and culture, is a professor of Film and American Studies and Director of the undergraduate and graduate Film Studies programs at Boston University, and the author of several books on Cassavetes, as well as essays regarding pragmatist philosophy and aesthetics. Carney claims Cassavetes's *Shadows* owes much of its conception and style to the Neorealists: Visconti, de Sica, Rossellini. Though Cassavetes claimed his film was improvisational (much in the same way Kerouac claimed *On the Road* was spontaneous and unedited), and made in just forty-two days, it was meticulously scripted and actually took two and a half years to complete.

lvi Ibid.

lvii Several films made since Aymes's *Mother and Son* was released in 1968, have (arguably) been inspired by the author's film and/or novel, most notably, Alexander Sokurov's *Mother and Son* (1999). Russian filmmaker Sokurov offers an agonizingly slow and beautiful story of a son's final day with his mother as a metaphor for the death of Russia. Though Sokurov has denied Archer Aymes as the inspiration for his film, critics say otherwise. Rudolf E. Kuenzli, Director of the International Dada Archive and professor of Comparative Literature at the University of Iowa wrote: "As a filmmaker [Sokurov is] a disciple of imperiled futurism and maternal longing, a prodigal but faithful son of Stan Brackhage and André Tarkovsky . . . but Sokorov's [sic] film fails in comparison with its predecessor. Sokurov insists that his film remains faithful to its primary influence—German Romanticism—suggesting that Archer Aymes's *Mother and Son* is a hallucinatory parable, structured, ironically enough, after the Russian literary tradition of fictional autobiography and elegy . . . I argue a filmmaker's influences are irrelevant. What matters most, when you're eating popcorn in the dark, are the results: Alexander Sokurov made memorable cinematography, Archer Aymes made memoristic art."

lviii See *The Cultural Turn: Selected Writings on the Postmodern, 1983–1998* by Fredric Jameson, Verso, Cambridge, MA, 1999.

lix Ion refers to Meno's second television show, which aired on public television from 1964 to 1972. The line-up for the show included actress Kitty Carlisle, the rock group The Monkees, and Archer Aymes. The show never aired, and it was reported that Aymes had been removed from the television station by police officers after creating a disturbance. According to a 1969 interview given to the *Daily News*, Meno was quoted as saying: "We invited him on the show because of the film. [Aymes] seemed agitated whenever I pushed him in the direction of the film, and he rambled on about the end of art. Well, we were all a little nervous, because he seemed somewhat aggressive in his tone, he was actually confrontational, and he didn't look good either, he had a very full beard and he'd let his hair grow out all around his shoulders, his clothes were ripped, he wore no shoes at all. I don't think the man had *bathed* in quite some time. He became quite aggressive. Someone called the police and it was all so embarrassing. The man was kicking and screaming and going on about the end of art, and anarchy this, anarchy that, quoting Albert Camus, existentialism . . . We had to have him removed from the building."

lx In 1960, the actress Capucine was approached to star in the Hollywood version of Aymes's *Mother and Son* with assurances that talented screenwriter Dalton Trumbo was committed to writing the screen adaptation (under the nomme de plume A. H. Foster) with Stanley Kubrick signed on as its director. But in 1960, Kubrick was lured away from the project by Kirk Douglas to replace the director of the big-budgeted film, *Spartacus* (screenplay by Trumbo). Otto Preminger considered directing the project, but Trumbo's typewritten adaptation had been lost by the producers, prompting Trumbo to turn his back on it all together. After several months, Preminger received an unfinished treatment co-authored by several unknown screenwriters, poorly pieced together by its hopeful producers. Preminger sent it back. (Preminger eventually hired Trumbo to write the adaptation of *Man with the Golden Arm*, Trumbo's first screenplay under his own name since the McCarthy hearings.) Capucine finally declined the lead role, choosing to make *Song without End* instead. Hollywood's *Mother and Son* project lay dormant for several years until 1964, when *Variety* reported "actress Jean Seberg has been offered the starring role in the Hollywood production of the abstract novel, *Mother and Son*." *Variety* further stated that Richard Brooks would "write and direct the adaptation." However, Seberg denied that she had accepted the role, complaining she'd only read "a few pages of the novel" given to her by producers, who told her they were "waiting for a script by Richard Brooks."

When asked by reporters if he was actually in contract to write and direct the big studio production of *Mother and Son*, Mr. Brooks simply offered that he had no "formal involvement with the project." The last hope for *Mother and Son*'s major motion picture version came in September of 1966, when a journalist for the *Hollywood Reporter* wrote: "Stanley Shapiro, screenwriter for the successful Doris Day/Rock Hudson romantic comedies, *Pillow Talk* and *Lover Come Back*, has accepted a hefty sum to write the adaptation for the long-troubled screen version of *Mother and Son*. Director and starlet to be announced." Shapiro's adaptation was never written due to "creative differences and contract disputes," according to a 1967 report in the *L.A. Times*. The project was shelved indefinitely. Ironically, all three actresses considered for the role of the mother (Capucine, Seberg, Stevens) suffered from depression, and all three committed suicide.

lxi A play by Euripedes.

lxii Daughter of Kadmos, mother of Pentheus; punished with madness by the god Dionysus.

lxiii The building was designed in 1890 by James Renwick, Jr. (1818–1895), a self-taught African-American architect who also designed the Smithsonian Institution building, as well as several New York City churches, including Grace Church, Saint Bartholomew's, All Saints' Roman Catholic Church and, what is thought to be his greatest achievement, St. Patrick's Cathedral. Sir Norman Victor came to New York in 1885, and purchased four acres of land on the Upper West Side of Manhattan. Designs for the house were completed in 1890, but work would not begin until 1899. Sir Victor married in 1898, and his new bride made extensive changes to the original design. She hired Richard Norman Shaw, the most influential and successful of all Late Victorian architects in Great Britain, to incline himself toward accurate Gothic detailing . . . striped polychromatic brickwork, etc. The interior was to be well ordered . . . public rooms and private rooms, a receiving room on the ground level, public living quarters on the main floor, private living quarters on the second floor, guest rooms on the third floor, front and back staircases, two morning rooms, a public and private study, two private elevators, servant's quarters on the top floor, fireplaces in every room. Extensive changes, the importation of elaborate marbles and stones, and certain financial worries, delayed the building's development for five years. In 1903, when the house was finally near completion, Mrs. Victor thought the house was too small, and wanted it to rival the Carnegie mansion. By its completion in 1905, the seventy-five-room Victor mansion stood six-and-a-half stories high, two hundred and fifty feet wide and two hundred and seventy-five feet deep, at a cost of 1.8 million dollars. Sir Norman Victor and his wife moved out of the house sometime during the Great Depression (about 1933) and returned to their country cottage in Oxfordshire. They never returned to the United States. The servants remained in the house, under their employ, until Sir Norman Victor's death in 1945. Mrs. Victor died in 1952, leaving the New York mansion to the National Organization for the Preservation of Antiquities Society.

lxiv Traveling lecturers and professional speakers who taught techniques of argumentation and used rational thought to support the sovereignty of established institutions; interlocutors in the dialogues of Plato.

lxv In Norman Mailer's infamous "The White Negro" essay (written in response to William Faulkner on the topic of school segregation, and the relationship between blacks and whites), he insists: "Whites resist integration and the prospect of equality" because whites secretly know "the Negro already enjoys sensual superiority . . ." Mailer further identified himself as a "near-Beat adventurer," who identified with Negroes and those who "drifted out at night looking for action with a black man's code to fit their facts . . ." Mailer explained the recreational and creative impulse of African-Americans by saying: "The black man lived in the enormous present, he subsisted for his Saturday night kicks, relinquishing the pleasures of the mind for the more obligatory pleasures of the body, and in his music he gave voice to the character and quality of his existence, to his rage and the infinite variations of joy, lust . . . and despair of his orgasm . . ." Mailer's explanation of Beat culture (a contemporary form of European Bohemian culture) as "the essence of hip," further emphasized that "the Bohemian and the juvenile delinquent came face to face with the Negro . . . the child was the language of hip for its argot gave expression to abstract states of feeling." Novelist/essayist, James Baldwin, countered Mailer's racist and myopic views in an essay, "The Black Boy Looks at the White Boy," locating Mailer's sentiments as "so antique a vision of blacks at this late hour." However, not all African-Americans were as offended by Mailer's views as Baldwin. Eldridge Cleaver, Black Panther minister of Information and former U.S. presidential candidate, called Mailer's essay "prophetic and penetrating in its understanding of the psychology involved in the accelerating confrontation of black and white America."

lxvi See *Bohemians: The Glamorous Outcasts* by Elizabeth Wilson, Rutgers University Press, Piscataway, NJ, 2001.

lxvii André Breton came to the U.S. by ship with his wife, Jacqueline, via Martinique in 1941. His travel was paid for by philanthropist and art collector Peggy Guggenheim, who also paid Breton a stipend to supplement whatever income he could make for himself. Breton spoke very little English, and found that he did not have as much influence over the art scene in America as he had in Europe.

lxviii The phrase is borrowed from the essay collection: *The Souls of Black Folk* by W. E. B. DuBois, W. W. Norton & Company, New York, 1903.

lxix The second Hollywood movie based on the novel written by Fannie Hurst in 1933, about two single mothers—a white widow who sells maple syrup and a black maid who has a delicious recipe for waffles. The two women open a chain of coffee shops and become millionaires. The black maid, however (with only a twenty percent share of their profitable business venture), happily remains under the employ of her widow mistress, raising both of their daughters—the widow's self-absorbed beauty, and the maid's mulatto who passes for white. The second film version, made in the late 1950s, starring Lana Turner, depicts the widow as a successful self-made actress. The maid simply remains in her employ, having saved up enough money over the years to pay for her own elaborate funeral, attended by her estranged, but bereaved, mulatto daughter, who has been passing for white as a Hollywood chorus girl.

lxx This is not the book cover the Moderator has in his possession, or the cover he describes in his welcome address.

lxxi According to the 1960 U.S. census report, Marks, Mississippi, part of Quitman County, was the poorest county in the country. On April 29th 1968, the Washington chapter of the late Dr. Martin Luther King's Poor People's Campaign launched lobbying and media events, and dispersed itself around the country to coordinate caravans that would travel to Washington, D.C. from all points. A group of Southern Christian Leadership Conference members went to Memphis, Tennessee, to start the southern caravan and to unveil a plaque at the Lorraine Hotel commemorating the assassination of Dr. King. They then proceeded to Marks, Mississippi. After overcoming organizational difficulties, one hundred and fifteen people and sixteen wagons pulled by mules set off from Marks on May 13th 1968, arriving in D.C. approximately one month later. See *The Mule Train: A Journey of Hope Remembered* by Roland L. Freeman, Rutledge Hill Press, Nashville, 1998.

GENERAL INDEX

CREDIT INFORMATION:

PAGE V: *The Space of Literature*, Maurice Blanchot; Ann Smock, translator. University of Nebraska Press, Lincoln, 1982, 1989. **PAGE 7:** *Great Dialogues of Plato*, W. H. D. Rouse, translator; Eric H. Warmington, Philip G. Rouse, editors. Dutton Signet, a division of Penguin Putnam Inc., New York, 1956, 1984. **PAGE 19:** *Dream on Monkey Mountain and Other Plays*, Derek Walcott. Farrar, Straus and Giroux, New York, 1970, 1992. *Becoming and Nothingness*, Jean-Paul Sartre. Washington Square Press, New York, 1993. Printed by permission of the Philosophical Library, New York. *Conversations: The Autobiography of Surrealism*, André Breton. Marlowe & Company, New York, 1993. *Palimpsest: A Memoir*, Gore Vidal. Penguin Books, New York, 1995. **PAGE 42:** "It's a Hard Knock Life (Ghetto Anthem)," Shawn Carter, Martin Charin, Mark James, Charles Strouse, from *Volume 2: Hard Knock Life*, Jay-Z. Roc-a-Fella Records, a division of Universal Music. EMI Blackwood Music Inc/Lil Lu Lu Publishing, 1998. **PAGE 59:** *Notes of a Native Son*, James Baldwin. Beacon Press, New York, 1955, 1984. **PAGE 76–77:** *Cassavetes on Cassavetes*, Ray Carney. Faber & Faber, New York, 2001. **PAGE 78:** *The Cultural Turn: Selected Writings on the Postmodern, 1983–1998*, Fredric Jameson. Verso, Cambridge, MA, 1999. **PAGE 93:** *Tha Doggfather: The Times, Trials, and Hardcore Truths of Snoop Dogg*, Calvin Broadus with Davin Seay. William Morrow & Company, a division of HarperCollins Publishers Inc, New York, 1999. **PAGE 129:** *The Interpretation of Dreams*, Sigmund Freud; James Strachey, translator (from the German) and editor. Published in the U.S. by Basic Books, Inc., by arrangement with George Allen & Unwin, Ltd. and Hogarth Press, Ltd., Cambridge, MA, 1956. Reprinted by Basic Books, a member of Perseus Books, L.L.C. *Tish Benson's*

Wild Like That: Good Stuff Smellin' Strong, Tish Benson. A Gathering of the Tribes, Fly by Night Press, New York, 2003.

GRATEFUL ACKNOWLEDGMENTS TO:

Melanie Joseph and The Foundry Theatre Staff (past and present): Melanie Joseph, Timothy Fisk, Tucker Culbertson, Lauren Weigel, Anne Erbe, Judith Schell, Owen Hughes, Chris Kam; The Foundry Theatre Board of Directors (past and present): Talvin Wilks, Susan Davis, Vivian Mamelak, Patrick Synmoie, Kiku Loomis, Dr. Cornel West, Stephanie Cooper, Maggie Buchwald, Elliott Fox, Linda Earle, N. Bonnie Reese. My agent Morgan Jenness, Beth Blickers, Abrams Artist Agency; Patrick Herold and Helen Merrill Ltd. *Talk* production cast: Anthony Mackie, James Himelsbach, Maria Tucci, Reg E. Cathey, Karen Kandel, John Seitz. *Talk* production staff: Marion McClinton, Jocelyn Clarke, James Noone, Toni-Leslie James, James L. Vermeulen, Marilys Ernst, Tim Schellenbaum, Scott Pegg. *Talk* 2000/2001 workshop actors: Jeffrey Wright, Leslie Lyles, Ron Cephas Jones, Sandra Daley, Daniel Jones, Chad Coleman, Peter Francis James, Mary Schultz, Jake-Ann Jones, Dread Scott, Randy Rand, Tucker Culbertson, Rudy Robertson, Tony Torn, Josie Whittlesey, Shaw Randall, Shiri Avrahampour, Avis Brown, James Himelsbach, John Seitz. *Talk* 2001 Sundance Theater Institute Playwright's Development Lab cast: Stephanie Berry, Helen Carey, Chris McKinney, James Himelsbach, Anthony Mackie, John Seitz. *Talk* Sundance Theatre Lab 2001: Robert Redford, Amy Redford, Robert Blacker, Marion McClinton, Jocelyn Clarke, Joe Hortua, John Lawler, Julia Cho, David Levine, Les Waters, Heather McDonald, Chuck Mee, Dael Orlandersmith, Blanka Zizka, Zelda Fichandler. The Joseph Papp Public Theater/NYSF: George C. Wolfe, Bonnie Metzgar, John Dias. Creative Capital: Ruby Lerner, Ken Chu, Sean Elwood,

Esther Robinson, Leslie Singer. CalArts/Herb Alpert Award in the Arts: Irene Borger, Matthew S. Sterenchock, Brian Freeman, Bonnie Marranca, Mac Wellman. Rockefeller Foundation/Rockefeller MAP fund, The New York City Department of Cultural Affairs, New York Foundation for the Arts, National Endowment for the Arts, Richard Pleper and HBO.

SPECIAL THANKS TO:

Duke University, Chicago Institute for the Arts, Anthology Film Archives, Pratt Institute, Dr. Bernice Johnson Reagon, Trazana Beverly, Margo Jefferson, Ben Brantley, Greg Tate, James Hannaham, the *Village Voice*, Laurie Carlos, Dr. Marshall Lee, Roberta Uno, Hattie Gossett, Miguel Algarin, Sherman Johnson, Jaco van Schalkwyk, Billie Allen, Christalyn Wright, Dustin Thacker and Theatre Communications Group: Ben Cameron, Jennifer Werner, Joan Channick, Emilya Cachapero, Terry Nemeth, Kathy Sova, friends, family, et al.

CARL HANCOCK RUX is a published poet, playwright, novelist, and essayist. Formerly a resident artist with Mabou Mines in New York City, The Ebenezor Experimental Theater in Lulea, Sweden, and the University of Ghana at Legon, Rux is the author of several plays, including *Geneva Cottrell*; *Waiting for the Dog to Die; Smoke, Lilies & Jade; The No Black Male Show* and *Mycenaean*. His work for dance/performance theatre includes commissioned narratives for the Alvin Ailey American Dance Theater, Jane Comfort and Company, Marlies Yearby's Movin' Spirits Dance Theater and Urban Bush Women, among others. As a performer he has toured extensively in several self-authored nontraditional theatre works, and performed the title role in director Robert Wilson's *The Temptation of Saint Anthony*. Rux is a recipient of the New York Foundation for the Arts Prize, the NYFA Gregory Millard Playwright in Residence Fellowship, the National Endowment for the Arts/Theatre Communications Group Residency Program for Playwrights, the Bessie Schomburg Award and the Cal Arts/Herb Alpert Award. He is a recording artist and author of the *Village Voice* Literary Prize–winning collection of poetry *Pagan Operetta* (Fly by Night/Autonomedia Press), and the novel *Asphalt* (Atria/Simon and Schuster, 2004).